A Management Guide for
Invasive Plants in Southern Forests

James H. Miller, Steven T. Manning, and Stephen F. Enloe

United States Department of Agriculture • Forest Service • Southern Research Station

General Technical Report SRS–131

Authors:

James H. Miller, Emeritus Research Ecologist, Forest Service, U.S. Department of Agriculture, Southern Research Station, Auburn University, AL 36849; **Steven T. Manning**, President, Invasive Plant Control, Inc., Nashville, TN 37204; and **Stephen F. Enloe**, Weed Management Specialist, Auburn University, Department of Agronomy, Auburn, AL 36849.

A Management Guide for Invasive Plants in Southern Forests

James H. Miller, Steven T. Manning,
and Stephen F. Enloe

Abstract

Invasions of nonnative plants into forests of the Southern United States continue to spread and include new species, increasingly eroding forest productivity, hindering forest use and management activities, and degrading diversity and wildlife habitat. This book provides the latest information on how to organize and enact prevention programs, build strategies, implement integrated procedures for management, and proceed towards site rehabilitation and restoration. Effective control prescriptions are provided for 56 nonnative plants and groups currently invading the forests of the 13 Southern States. A companion book, "A Field Guide for the Identification of Invasive Plants in Southern Forests," (Miller and others 2010 (slight revision 2012)) includes information and images for accurate identification of these invasive plants.

Keywords: Alien plants, exotic weeds, forest noxious plants, invasive exotic plants, invasive nonindigenous plants.

Acknowledgments

The clarity and accuracy of descriptions of integrated invasive plant management programs, tools, treatments, and prescriptions have been measurably improved by the sizable and appreciated reviews of these experts: Chris Evans, Coordinator, River to River Cooperative Weed Management Area, Marion, IL; Nancy Fraley, Coordinator, Southeast Exotic Plant Management Team, U.S. Department of the Interior, National Park Service, Asheville, NC; Patrick Minogue, Assistant Professor of Silviculture, the University of Florida, North Florida Research and Education Center, Quincy, FL; David Moorhead, Professor and Codirector, Center for Invasive Species and Ecosystem Health, the University of Georgia, Tifton, GA; and Matt Nespeca, Executive Director, Conservation Land Company, Inc., Charleston, SC. Layout and photo management were by Erwin B. Chambliss, Forest Service, U.S. Department of Agriculture, Southern Research Station, Auburn University, AL.

All plant images by James H. Miller and posted on Bugwood.org, with crucial contributions by:

Chuck Bargeron, University of Georgia, Tifton, GA, Bugwood.org
Ted Bodner, copyrighted by the University of Georgia Press for "Forest Plants of the Southeast and Their Wildlife Uses" (used by permission)
Paul Bolstad, University of Minnesota, Bugwood.org
Patrick Breen, Oregon State University, Department of Horticulture, Corvallis, OR, Bugwood.org
John D. Byrd, Mississippi State University, Bugwood.org
Charles T. Bryson, USDA Agricultural Research Service, Southern Weed Science Research Unit, Stoneville, MS, Bugwood.org
Gary Buckingham, USDA Agricultural Research Service, Bugwood.org
Erwin B. Chambliss, USDA Forest Service, Southern Research Station, Auburn, AL
Terry Clason, Louisiana USDA Natural Resources and Conservation Service, Alexandria, LA
Steve Dewey, Utah State University Extension, Logan, UT, Bugwood.org
Chris Evans, River to River Cooperative Weed Management Area, Marion, IL, Bugwood.org
John Everest, Department of Agronomy & Soils, Auburn University, Auburn, AL
Wilson Faircloth, USDA Agricultural Research Service, Dawson, GA
Nancy Fraley, U.S. Department of the Interior, National Park Service, Asheville, NC
Great Smoky Mountains National Park, Resource Management Archive, USDI National Park Service, Gatlinburg, TN, Bugwood.org
Karl Haagsma, USDA Agricultural Research Service, Youngstown, OH
Newt Hardie, The Kudzu Coalition, Spartanburg, SC
Jane Hargeaves, Progressive Associates, Asheville, NC
Dick Henry, Bellwether Solutions, Concord, NH
Ben Jackson, University of Georgia, Bugwood.org
Michael Jordan, Alabama Department of Environmental Management, Montgomery, AL
Steven Katovich, USDA Forest Service, Forest Health Protection, Bugwood.org
John Klepac, USDA Forest Service, Southern Research Station, Auburn, AL
Nancy Loewenstein, School of Forestry and Wildlife Sciences, Auburn University, Auburn, AL
John Lyddon, Star Hill Solutions, Inc., Half Moon Bay, CA
Steven T. Manning, Invasive Plant Control, Inc., Nashville, TN, Bugwood.org
Dennis Markwardt, Texas Department of Transportation, Austin, TX
John McGuire, Westervelt Wildlife Services, Tuscaloosa, AL
Leslie J. Mehrhoff, University of Connecticut, Storrs, CT, Bugwood.org
Dana Mitchell, USDA Forest Service, Southern Research Station, Auburn, AL
David J. Moorhead, Center for Invasive Species and Ecosystem Health, University of Georgia, Tifton, GA, Bugwood.org
Fred Nation, Weeks Bay National Estuarine Research Reserve, Weeks Bay, AL
Ron Nehrig, USDA Agricultural Research Service, Youngstown, OH
Ohio State Weed Lab Archive, The Ohio State University, Bugwood.org
Christopher Oswalt, USDA Forest Service, Southern Research Station, Forest Inventory and Analysis, Knoxville, TN
Outdoors Magic, http://www.outdoorsmagic.com/
Pennsylvania Department of Conservation and Natural Resources—Forestry Archive, Harrisburg, PA, Bugwood.org
Corrie Pieterson, School of Forest Resources and Conservation, University of Florida, Gainesville, FL
John M. Randall, The Nature Conservancy, University of California, Davis, CA, Bugwood.org
Jeff Sibley, Department of Horticulture, Auburn University, Auburn, AL
Forest and Kim Starr, U.S. Geological Survey, Bugwood.org
Spraying Systems, Inc., Wheaton, IL
Gena Todia, Wetland Resources Environmental Consulting, Fairhope, AL
USDA Forest Service Archive, USDA Forest Service, Bugwood.org
Dale Wade, Rx Fire Doctor, Bugwood.org
Waldrum Specialties, Inc., Southhampton, PA
Government of Western Australia, Department of Agriculture and Food, 3 Baron-Hay Court, South Perth, WA
Chad Zorn, Lostwood WMD Complex, Kenmare, ND

Plant names from:

USDA Natural Resources Conservation Service's Plants Database: http://plants. usda.gov with recent published modifications.

Contents

continued

---

* Headings in gold italics denote sidebars in text.

Contents (continued)

continued

---

* Headings in gold italics denote sidebars in text.

Contents (continued)

Introduction

Only recently has the extent of invasive plant occupation in the Southern United States and elsewhere in the world been realized. Coming rather quickly in the past 10 to 50 years, the extent and spread of nonnative plant species has taken many people by surprise, and it is still not comprehended by most citizens and policymakers. One thing is starkly apparent, however, forest, preserve, and right-of-way managers and landowners need to act fast to stop the rapid encroachment of nonnative invasive plants, eradicate infestations, and restore native communities.

Forest overstory, mid-story, and ground layer replaced by invasive species.

Chinese wisteria, Chinese privet, Chinese lespedeza, and Japanese honeysuckle invading forest lands.

It was only in 1999 that President Clinton issued the executive order defining an "invasive species" and mandating specific Federal actions. The definition of an invasive species in that order is: (1) a species that is nonnative (or alien) to the ecosystem under consideration, such as the Southeast; and (2) whose introduction causes or is likely to cause economic or environmental harm or harm to human health (Executive Order 13112, signed February 3, 1999, by President Clinton).

Thus, a plant invader is any plant species that occurs outside its area of origin and that has become established, can reproduce, and can spread without cultivation and causes harm. Prevention, management, and strategies for control of nonnative plants of the Southeast are addressed in this book and their identification in the companion volume, "A Field Guide for the Identification of Invasive Plants in Southern Forests" (Miller and others 2010). Two other invaluable books for identifying and managing invasive plants in Florida, which are not covered here, are "Identification and Biology of Nonnative Plants in Florida's Natural Areas" (Langeland and others 2008) and "Control of Non-Native Plants in Natural Areas of Florida" (Langeland and Stocker 2009).

The damages and impacts of nonnative invasive plants have not been completely determined, but the following are generally recognized:

Nonnative invasive plants

- Limit or stop productive land management and regeneration of forests and grasslands.

- Displace and permanently decrease biodiversity and wildlife habitat.

- Alter vital ecological processes such as soil formation, watershed function, and pollination of native plants.

- Limit land access for recreation such as hiking, fishing, hunting, and bird watching.

- Produce overabundant pollen that causes widespread allergenic reactions in humans.

- Present extreme fire hazards to forests, preserves, and homes.

- Can be poisonous to humans and livestock.

- Harbor plant diseases.

- Cause psychological anxiety through a sense of the inability to control our surroundings.

Not all nonnative plants are invasive, and a few are among our most valued crops, e.g., wheat, barley, oats, and a Native American introduction from Mesoamerica, corn. Other nonnative grasses are the mainstay forage species, although most of these are invasive in forests or forest openings, such as Bermudagrass [*Cynodon dactylon* (L.) Pers.], bahiagrass (*Paspalum notatum* Flueggé), and tall fescue [*Schedonorus phoenix* (Scop.) Holub]. Plant breeding programs over the past 100 years have yielded numerous varieties of each crop and forage species that give landowners plants with increased productivity, useable yields, and tolerance to a wider range of growing conditions and predators.

John McGuire

Cogongrass burns unnaturally hot.

2

Over the past 50 years, the explosion in the number of ornamental and horticultural species and abundant varieties has yielded benefits to many aspects of modern society, such as landscape beautification and rapid-growing shade trees and shrubs, but have taken their toll on our natural ecosystems. The social costs of annual maintenance control of these introduced invasive species have skyrocketed in our yards, parks, green spaces, and along rights-of-way as well as forests, grasslands, and wildlands.

Nonnative plants become invasive for many reasons. The following are among the traits that help nonnative species establish and spread:
- Early introduction in the 1700s and 1800s as ornamentals or forages, resulting in a long period of spread, hybridization, and adaptation (Hundreds of thousands of small farmers planted ornamentals around their houses, and the plants remained after the great exodus in the late 1800s and early 1900s to cities.)
- Rapid early growth rates that outpace native cohorts
- Few native predators and a resiliency to predation by insects, pathogens, and mammals
- Production of abundant fruit and seed at a young age
- Seed that is readily spread by wind, water, birds, and mammals
- Seed that can remain viable in the soil for 1 year and even up to decades
- Roots or rhizomes that persist and resprout after topkill following herbicide applications, cutting, or burning and that grow outward to yield intensified and dense infestations
- Capability to establish and spread in sites of periodic disturbance, such as along ever expanding forest edges, on rights-of-way, along stream and river banks, and in abandoned crop and pasture lands

Nonnative shrub production.

Old homestead with wisteria and privet.

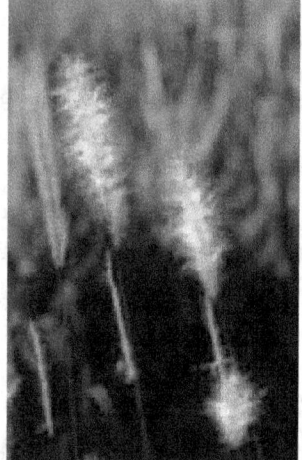
Cogongrass seedheads.

Bamboo rhizomes and roots.

- Capability to adapt and spread in a new site through a "set-and-wait" strategy until conditions are suitable
- Wide tolerance to shade, drought, soil conditions, and flooding that gives a decided advantage over native plants
- Capability of forming exclusive (or limited species) dense infestations through their high amount of leaf area that is often evergreen or appears earlier in spring and sheds later in fall compared to native species
- Capability of suppressing other plant seed germination and growth by releasing allelopathic chemicals (through the invasive plant's foliage and roots)
- Alter biogeochemical cycles and soil micobial communities that favor invaders over native plants

The more of these traits a nonnative species might have, the greater its likelihood of success in establishing itself and spreading, as well as resisting control and eradication.

Recently escaped plants can remain at low levels of scattered occurrence known as the "lag phase" but then come into an era of rapid increasing spread. Invasive traits can be enhanced through hybridization with native or nonnative plants of the same genus. There are nonnative plants at every stage of invasion in the Southeast, while across the region none are yet at the "maximum occupation" phase. Many currently "naturalized" plants in the early lag phase will likely become invasive due to selective adaptation and hybridization as well as increased disturbed habitat for establishment.

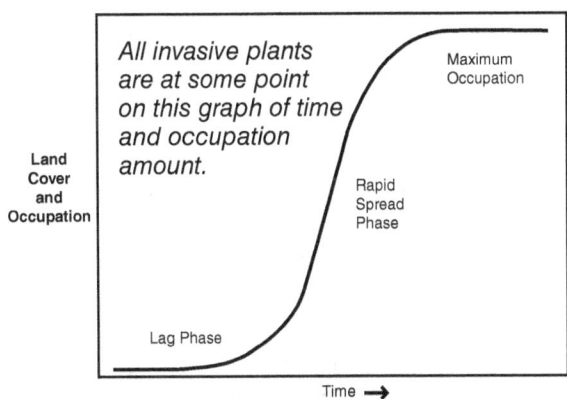

The objective of this book is to provide useful information on current management strategies and procedures for 56 recognized plants that have invaded forests, natural areas, pastures, rights-of-way, orchards, grasslands, and wetlands of the Eastern United States. This book also covers the principles of invasion and how we can organize, plan, and enact prevention and management programs.

General Principles for Managing Nonnative Invasive Plants

Three overarching concepts provide powerful ways to get organized and counter invasive plant takeovers: adaptation, collaboration, and restoration.

Adaptive Management Cycle for an area

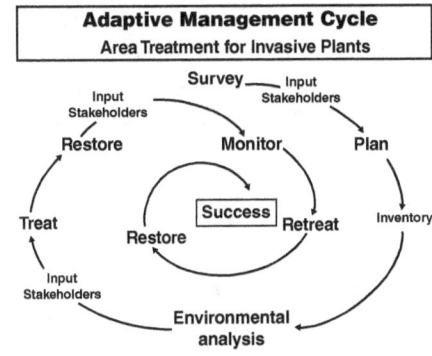

- **Adaptation**, or adaptive resource management, generally refers to a community shared process of self-conscious learning by doing. The process involves goal setting, gaining experience and research findings, and monitoring actions and outcomes with rapid incorporation of new knowledge into refined goals and actions. It is a corporate cyclical process of learning, adapting, and managing. It is a process of optimal decisionmaking in the face of uncertainty, with an aim of reducing uncertainty over time by monitoring results of actions and careful adjustments to improve outcomes. We do not have all the solutions for fighting the invasion of nonnative plant species, but, by pooling our information resources, we can learn together how to improve our approaches and treatments. We must make full use of print and Web resources, and we can become even more effective by paying attention to new and forthcoming information (see "Resource Information" on page 103).

- **Collaboration** with adjacent and area landowners is essential because invasive plant infestations most often occur across ownership and political boundaries. For greatest effectiveness, we must develop and use communication networks to link local, county, State, and regional programs.

- **Restoration** of infested lands to healthy and productive ecosystems must be our guiding objective. We only can be successful with eradication, control, and containment of invasive plants through the establishment of desirable and useful plants that protect soil, produce needed resources and habitats, and safeguard our lands from a resurgence of invasive plants. We must identify, establish, and culture resistant and resilient plant communities on rehabilitated and restored lands, and then we must monitor these communities for the first possible signs of returning invasive plants. Restoration approaches for most invasive plants are just being developed and will require adaptive management cycles to perfect.

Cooperative planning is critical.

4

Regional and State Program Elements for Invasive Plant Management

Required program elements are:

- Cooperative knowledge networks that link stakeholders, land managers, scientists, policymakers, and political representatives at the national, regional, State, multicounty, and county levels and that provide real time information and connectivity. Critical to how well the network functions are the timely actions and communications by all the people involved, whether they are working in voluntary, delegated, or assigned roles.

- Collaborative strategies and programs for spread prevention through: (1) improved laws, policies, and public education; (2) promotion of new corporate and personal ethics to not sell, buy, and plant invasive plants; (3) sanitization of personnel, equipment, and animals that move from or among infested sites; and (4) prohibition against the sale and transport of contaminated products such as extracted native plants, potted plants, hay, pine straw, fill dirt and rock, and mulch.

- Effective and efficient early detection and rapid response networks to identify and map high-risk sites and new introductions, verify the invasive species, communicate to others about the newly identified sites, eradicate the infestations, and restore plant communities resistant to reinvasion

- Creation and maintenance of a Web-accessible survey, inventory, and mapping system to corporately track existing and spreading invasions, e.g., Southeast Exotic Pest Plant Council's Early Detection and Distribution Mapping System (http://se-eppc.org/). Such a system with retrievable maps is invaluable for identifying and communicating information about zones of high infestations, advancing fronts, outliers, and weed-free zones. As an example of the value of current survey results, the Forest Inventory and Analysis (FIA) unit of the USDA Forest Service, Southern Research Station, works with State partners to develop the Invasive Plant database http://srsfia2.fs.fed.us/nonnative_invasive/Southern_Nonnative_Invasives.htm. Data on Japanese honeysuckle (*Lonicera japonica* Thunb.) and nonnative privets (*Ligustrum* spp.) along with 51 other invasive plants in the 13 States of the southern forest

Occupation of Japanese honeysuckle and nonnative privets (March 2008)

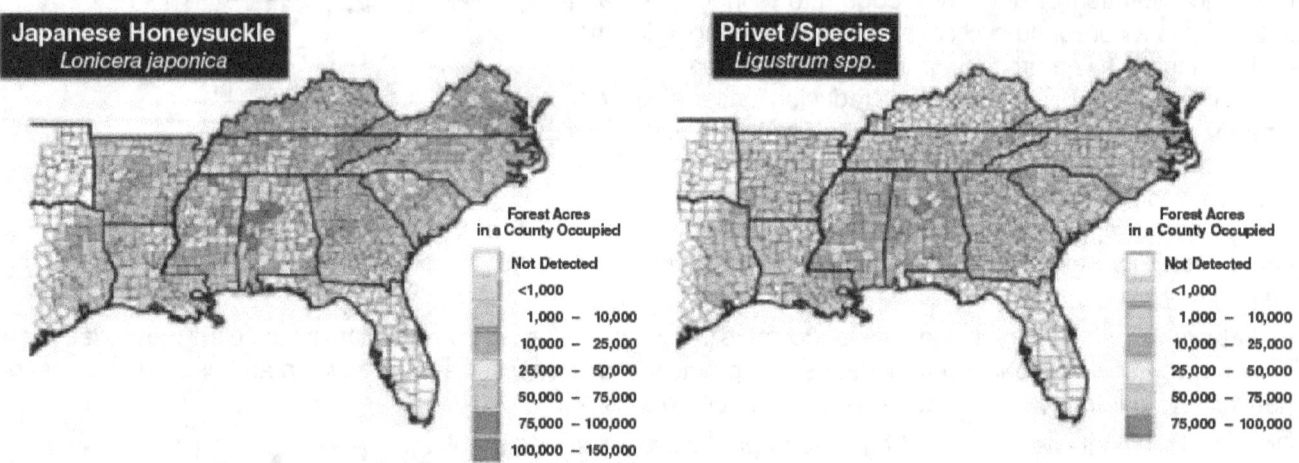

region of the United States are posted on the periodically updated Web site. Updating cycles for this FIA invasive plant survey depend on the survey activities within individual States, with most cycles updated in part annually. Current occupation maps and areas are posted at http://www.invasive.org/fiamaps/ and at http://srsfia2.fs.fed.us/data_center/data_mapping.shtml.

- Formulation of coordinated control, containment, and eradication programs, including cycles of integrated treatments along with monitoring and corporate sharing of both successes and mistakes. As shown in the maps of occupation for Japanese honeysuckle and privets, a coordinated multi-State control and eradication program that targets outliers is necessary to stop the spread, contain advancing fronts, and protect special habitats in severely infested zones. Spread prevention programs are also a crucial element through public education, as are regional biological control programs for widespread severe nonnative invasive plants.

Zones of invasion and the needed coordinated actions

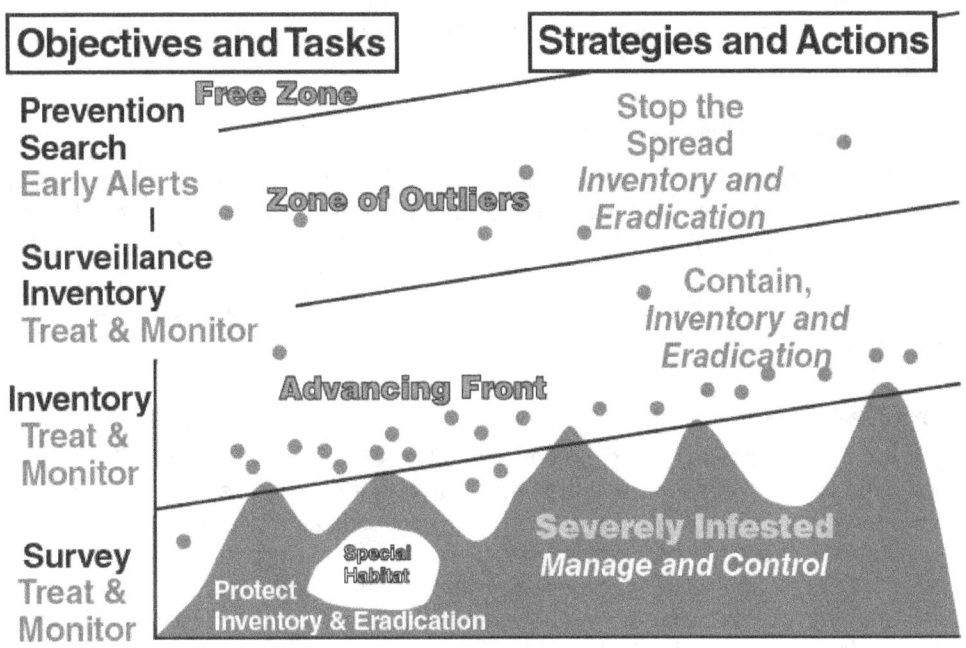

- Restoration treatments to dovetail with control and eradication efforts that guarantee suppression of invasive plants and maintenance of ecosystem functions and services. Adaptive information cycles are especially needed in this rapidly developing field of ecosystem restoration. Continued surveillance and monitoring with timely reintervention are essential for successful rehabilitation and restoration.
- Dedicated invasive plant research and research syntheses are demanded, followed with rapid technology transfer of findings through effective knowledge networks with feedback from the field on additional research needs.

The spread of invasive plants from State to State means that every State must have in place an invasive plant management plan. The plans should share common elements that assure regional protection, including working elements and programs for adaptive collaborative restoration. The plans must permanently implant adaptive management cycles that foster learning about how to control invasive plants, as well as sharing advances in knowledge with all stakeholders in every State. To best constrain invasions and restore eco-services, regional, State, and local strategies and actions should be unified and readily shared through collaborative networks.

Strategies for Confronting a Spreading Invader

The spread and occupation of an invasive plant can be stopped only through regional and State plans and programs that are effectively implemented at the local level. Draw lines on maps to define zones of occupation severity and show areas where different strategies should be employed.

Managing Outlier Areas

Outlier (or satellite) infestations exist beyond highly infested areas due to long distance movement of plants or plant reproductive parts. Outlier infestations must be detected and eradicated early if containment is to be successful. Early detection rests with public education as well as organized search and surveillance efforts and strong reporting networks. Movement of contaminated equipment and materials must be effectively prevented to stop new outlier infestations from being established.

Managing the Advancing Front of Invasive Infestations

All infestations along the advancing front must be found, mapped, and documented through intensive search and surveillance programs. The search and surveillance programs must include all ownerships. To stop seed dispersal from worsening the situation, treatments must be timely and persistent. For all work near or inside infested areas, extra care must be taken to ensure sanitation of equipment and personnel to prevent spread. Special habitats of rare plants and animals within the advancing front zone should be carefully treated to save from ultimate loss. The front must be held and then pushed back.

Managing Severely Infested Areas

Surveys employing sampling techniques are required to quantify the acres of infestation. Concerted programs in cooperation with landowners with funded assistance are needed to fully implement, support, and maintain management programs in severely infested zones. Equipment and personnel sanitation as well as quarantines of product movement out of severely infested areas must be strictly regulated to prevent both short- and long-distance movement of plants and reproductive parts. Any forest and nursery product movement must be monitored for contamination. Special habitats of rare plants and animals must be safeguarded from destruction and restored using special techniques. People's homes must be safeguarded against wildfire by highly flammable invasive plants.

A Shift in Mindset Must Occur Followed by Actions

Successful management of nonnative invasive plants will require a shift in mindset. The number of species, their area of occupation, and their spread are drastically increasing—a threat that demands new knowledge and approaches by land managers at a new level of regional, State, and local cooperation. Weed management has been a growing science and practice with intensive agriculture and horticulture, while weed populations, becoming toughened by hybridization and new introductions, are spreading across land uses. Forestry, right-of-way, park, and preserve managers should borrow and modify control techniques from agriculture and from one another. Accurate identification skills of both invasive and native plants are required for precise management. New tools, machines, products, and techniques should be acquired and mastered in a timely manner to effectively confront the invasions, beat them back, and restore lands. Mindset changes also should occur at all levels of policy and agency jurisdictions to complement and augment private and local efforts.

Invasive plants are still sold like sweet autumn virginsbower (Clematis terniflora DC).

The three logistical areas where a mindset shift could result in more effective management of invasive plants are in recognizing the need for more comprehensive and integrated planning, better and more timely preparation, and a heightened resolve and persistence. All ownership, area, and site management plans should include goals and actions addressing prevention, eradication, and control of invasive infestations; but such plans are incomplete if they do not lead to site rehabilitation or restoration. Management activities such as timber harvesting, stand thinning, prescribed burning, and road and firebreak maintenance should include an integrated plan for minimizing entry and spread of invasive plants and planned reaction to any new infestations.

Preparation always has been critical to forest, roadway, and natural area managers and landowners. As invasive plant populations increase in size and density, land managers and owners must be willing to employ and deploy new concepts, tools, and materials. Preparation entails seeking the very latest information on invasive plant identification, prevention and control methods, and rehabilitation and restoration techniques. It also means finding reliable sources of noncontaminated fill dirt and rock, seed, and mulch for soil stabilization. To fully prepare for rehabilitation and restoration, managers and landowners may need to purchase newly available native seeds, planting tools and equipment, landscape fabrics and fiber mats for stabilization, and also may need to seek professional services.

Without persistence, all efforts to control and rehabilitate infested lands will be lost. To nurture a healthy native or noninvasive community of plants, managers and landowners will need to persist in a regime that includes timed treatments and retreatments as well as tenacious follow through. This will need to be followed by years of site monitoring for reappearance of the prior or new invasive plant species.

Principles to Follow

- Never plant recognized invasive plants. Seek information on whether or not a plant is invasive before you purchase it (for lists and descriptions of invasive plants, go to www.invasive.org/weeds).

Locate sources of noncontaminated materials for soil stabilization and road construction.

- Detect invasive plants early through active surveillance of your lands. Map and mark locations of the invasive plants you find. Apply and document eradication treatments and monitor their effectiveness, retreating as needed. If treatments do not work, research ways to improve current treatments or find more effective alternatives.

- If you detect several invasive plants, prioritize your treatment by targeting the worst of the plants first. The worst plant may not be the plant that has infested your land the most, i.e., has the highest level of infestation. In many cases, the worst plant may be the plant that occupies the least territory but has the greatest potential for spreading. You should manage your fight against several detected species by balancing eradication of first entries of high-priority invasive plants with persistent treatment of extensive infestations (see www.invasive.org/south/ for a regional list of High Priority Invasive Species of Southern Forests and Grasslands).

- To prevent spread of invasive species outward from your property, perform road maintenance, timber harvest, and site preparation starting from the boundary of the infested area and working inward, from areas that are not infested to those that are. To prevent the spread of invasive species by contaminated equipment and personnel, postpone all management activities until you have suppressed or eradicated invasive plants from the site, or be prepared for the consequences of wider occupation. Always inspect and clean equipment before moving to another site.

Invasive plant strategies and programs ultimately depend upon the eradication and restoration of one infestation at a time at the local level and preventing new entries. Following these principles will greatly increase the chances of success.

Considerations in Developing a Site-Specific Plan

Answering the following questions will help you develop a plan that considers appropriate tools, timelines, costs, and outcomes.

What Is the Long-Term Plan for the Site?

Control methods can change dramatically based on the site's planned uses. For example, if the long-term plan is to keep the site cleared of all tall vegetation, then a less selective and less expensive approach can be used. If you need to protect indefinitely a site that contains many desirable or rare species, then consider a more selective long-term treatment and monitoring plan.

What Is the Need for Selectivity?

Selectivity means targeting invasive plants while minimizing damage to neighboring native plants. You can control specific plant species with a selective herbicide, or you can apply a nonselective herbicide selectively to treat only targeted invasive plants. As an example, you can use a broadcast herbicide on a prairie that is 99 percent invasive grasses. In some cases, the native soil seed bank will reestablish itself. If the prairie has been manipulated for many years, you may need to seed with native grasses. If the prairie contains a wide variety of native species intermixed with targeted nonnative species, you must choose a more selective herbicide or application method as well as burning and other rehabilitation treatments.

What Is the Intensity of Infestation?

The intensity of infestation is determined by the relative area and height of occupation, the infestation's age, the size and growth form of the invasive species, and the longevity of the invasive species' viable seeds or other propagules in the soil. These factors can dramatically affect the methods, timing, persistence, and costs of control and site rehabilitation. For example, you'll need to spend considerable time and effort treating an invasive multi-stemmed tree that has grown at high infestation levels, has grown on the site for a decade or more, and has long-lived residual seeds. You'll need less time and effort for scattered low-growing annual invaders with few residual seeds.

The target plant's size will dictate your treatment methods and limit application options. For example, if you have a high infestation of large Chinese privet (*L. sinense* Lour.) under a desirable hardwood overstory, you'll need to use methods appropriate for woody plant control that safeguard the hardwoods. On the other hand, if the privet is 1 to 2 years old or has been cut to resprout, you can more easily apply foliar applications of a nonselective herbicide during the dormant season—meaning you'll spend less time and herbicide and, thereby, save both effort and cost.

How Does Timing Affect Control Methods?

Understanding the life cycle of invasive plants helps the landowner, manager, and applicator select the optimum time for applying control treatments as well as revegetation actions. If you know the annual cycle of growth initiation, flowering and fruiting, drought responses, and periods of dormancy, you can plan the most effective approach. By applying herbicides, burning, and cutting at the appropriate stage in a plant's seasonal cycle, you can increase effectiveness and selectivity as well as reduce the need for additional retreatments. Other timing issues concern availability of labor and contract applications, number of treatments necessary in a season, and access periods for wetlands, high-elevation sites, parks, and military reservations.

What Type of Labor Will Work on the Site?

In-house, contract, and volunteer labor all have different strengths and distinct disadvantages. In some States, volunteers can apply herbicide treatments, but in most places, volunteers use only manual or mechanical control methods suitable for small infestations. In-house and contract workers often are the best trained in knowing how to handle larger infestations that require special equipment, precise herbicide applications, and other approaches presented in this guide.

How Important Is Cost?

The cost of a project is directly related to treatment method, intensity of infestation, plants and areas that need safeguarding, and availability of resources. Cost-share and incentive programs can decrease costs for the landowner, but the number and years of retreatment might be restrictive. Once you formulate a plan, make careful estimates of your costs in light of realistic objectives. Once you enact a plan, understand that disruption in scheduled treatments can cause major setbacks and even loss of your prior work. If you use ineffective treatments, like only cutting woody invasive plants without applying herbicide to the stumps, you can accrue large costs over the long run. Using only the most efficient methods is a wise investment in safeguarding a natural heritage for future generations.

Elements and Tasks of an Invasive Plant Management Program

Elements and Tasks

1. **Make a plan.**
2. **Prevent entry and spread.**
3. **Make a map of locations.**
4. **Eradicate, control or contain, and monitor results.**
5. **Rehabilitate, restore, or reclaim treated lands.**

Persistently sticking to a plan of adaptive and collaborative restoration is the only successful strategy for safeguarding land access, productivity, native plants, and suitable habitats for wildlife.

1. Make a plan. Base your planned treatments on stated objectives and the best information, then schedule and acquire resources that support your plan, devise a timeline for implementation of your plan's action items, and add some "wiggle room" for contingencies. Devise both a short- or long-term plan to include both specific infestation treatment regimes and ideas for how these fit into a general land management plan. Your maps of infestation locations and priority ratings of invasive species will assist the planning process.

An eradication and rehabilitation program for specific invasive plant infestations usually requires several years of treatments and many more years of surveillance to check for rhizome and root resprouts, seed germination, or new invaders. Newer infestations and smaller plants require much less time than extensive and dense infestations.

During the treatment and retreatment phase, you must take steps to safeguard, promote, or establish desirable vegetation. To effectively combat plant invasions and restore lands, you will need to carefully plan for each step in the program by incorporating primary and contingency schedules of enactment. You should project a minimum of 4 years and up to 10 years for older infestations and when less than maximum effective treatments are used. You can use short-term plans to target specific areas, but you will need a long-term management plan for an increasingly invaded landscape. You must consider surrounding lands, particularly the degree of current infestation in those lands as well as the invasive plant management programs the owners and managers of those lands have in place. You must also consider emerging State funding assistance programs.

2. Prevent entry and spread. Do not plant invasives such as those covered in this book, others listed in the appendix "Nonnative Invasive Plant Species Not to be Used or Recommended for Wildlife Food Plots nor Bird and Butterfly Viewing Gardens," and those on your State's noxious and invasive plant lists. For wildlife food plots, soil stabilization, and ornamentals, plant only native plants of local origin when possible or noninvasive alternatives.

- Educate yourself, employees, and other users of your land about the invasive plants that pose major threats and how to prevent their entry. Learn how to identify both invasive and native plants in your area. The more native plants that you can identify, the easier you will spot the "plants out of place."
- Sanitation procedures to prevent the spread of invasives. Require those who work, hunt, and recreate on your lands, to minimize invasive plant spread by following these procedures when working in or near infested lands:
  - Inspect the site and infestation before operations, especially noting the presence or absence of invasive plant fruit, seed heads, or spore clusters under climbing fern (*Lygodium* spp.) leaves. The absence of any of these propagules means that less stringent sanitation procedures will be required. When they are present and you are working in or near the infestation, maximum sanitation techniques should be followed to prevent spread.

– When possible, avoid driving vehicles, mowers, all-terrain vehicles (ATVs), or spray equipment through infestations in seed or fruit, especially late-flowering cogongrass [*Imperata cylindrical* (L.) Beauv.], and musk thistle (*Carduus nutans* L.). This is a very common means of spread for many species.

– Brush and wipe all seeds and debris from clothes, boots, socks, and personal protective equipment. Avoid wearing cuffed pants where seed may collect. Remove seeds from boot laces and soles before moving between infested sites. Carry large contractor-size refuse bags to stand in while brushing and removing seeds or place contaminated gear within the bag for careful cleaning at a designated location.

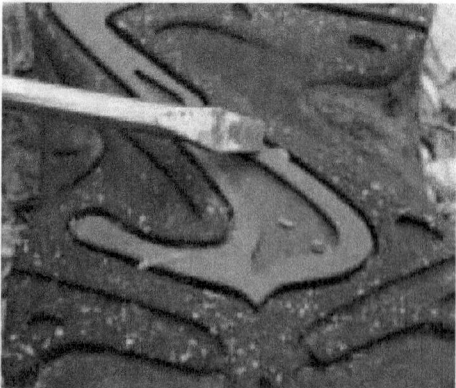
Seeds lodged in shoe sole.

– When working in invasive plant infestations, thoroughly clean motorized equipment, especially the undercarriage and tire surfaces, where seed and plant parts are often inadvertently caught and transported. Pressure washers can be used in combination with a narrow spade, scraper, and

Invasive seeds stick to mower tire.

Clean seeds and plants from equipment with pressure washer.

Wilson Faircloth

Cogongrass seeds on tractor radiator.

Excess grease traps seeds.

stiff brush to remove mud, soil, and debris. The undercarriage, radiator front, and engine compartments must be inspected and washed when suspected contaminates are present. Remove excess grease and oil that trap and carry seeds, fruits, and spores. Modify vehicles and equipment in ways that will prevent buildup of debris or use the most appropriate vehicle that has the least potential for contamination.

Invasive plants hitchhike on mowers.

- When moving cut invasive plants that have fruits and seeds offsite such as to a burn pile, always cover loads or bag before transport.

- Monitor burn pile areas for new seedlings as the fire may not consume or kill all seeds. Also, monitor any designated decontamination sites for seedlings.

- Sometimes sanitation seems almost impossible when dealing with invasive spore-forming species such as invasive climbing ferns, where spores are not easily seen. Avoid entering or working in invasive climbing fern infestations when spore clusters under special leaves are present. If entry is unavoidable, complete sanitation of all equipment, clothing, and workers is necessary to prevent potential spread. Plan entries into climbing fern infestations when spores are not present, which is October to November in the temperate parts of the region.

- Use only noncontaminated fill materials, mulches, and seeds. Inspect material sources at the site of origin for indications of contamination by invasive plants growing on or near the area.

- Regularly inspect areas where offsite fill materials have been used and areas used by visitors and lessees.

Cogongrass-infested borrow pit.

- Be careful not to disturb areas where there is a high probability of invasion. Most land disturbing activities raise the potential for establishment of aggressive plant invaders, especially when the invaders occur nearby.

- Most likely points of entry that need high-priority search and surveillance are:

  ◆ Lands adjacent to lands you do not own, highways, county roads, and utility rights-of-way and their edges and fencerows, especially after new construction or maintenance activities
  ◆ Internal roads, trails, and fire lines
  ◆ Lands next to streams, rivers, and lake shores, especially after recent flooding or high-flow periods
  ◆ Recently prepared and seeded wildlife food plots
  ◆ Harvested, thinned, burned, or storm-damaged areas during the years following disturbance

Road maintenance can spread invasive plants.

Cogongrass invading from transmission line right-of-way.

Invasive plants spread along internal road shoulders

Dormant cogongrass

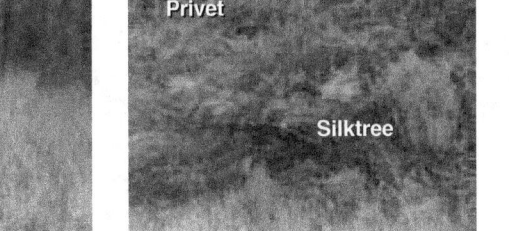

Privet

Silktree

Cogongrass

Invasive plant seeds move along streams.

3. Make a map and monitor results of locations. Identify invasive plant location sites at risk, and denote treatments and their outcomes. You must positively identify those invasive plants that are present and those poised to enter from adjacent lands, determine their locations and abundance, and record this information on a sketch map or Geographic Information System (GIS) map. Gain their Global Positioning System (GPS) locations when possible. Make the locations easy to find again by marking them with plastic flags. Monitor the locations through repeated visits and record progress or the lack of it. Agencies should map as many acres as possible with the dollars available before investing in unorganized treatments of extensive invasions, while new entries of severe invasives should be tackled early.

The search, survey, Inventory, monitor, and surveillance method—Using the four-option *Search, Survey, Inventory, Monitor, and Surveillance* method, hereafter referred to as SSIMS, will help you map, monitor, and track treatments with their results at several scales.

Invasive plants can be transported on wildlife food-plot equipment.

- *The first SSIMS option is searching.* Start by looking at the most likely points of entry, like along roads and especially near bridges, and record any occurrence of invasive plants you find in such areas. Then widen your search as time and resources permit.

- *The second option is survey.* Surveys are used to sample large areas where search procedures have found numerous infestations that are too many to inventory individually. Surveys are also used to examine large tracks when the amount of invasion is unknown and access is difficult. By systematically locating plots or by band sampling across the landscape, you can record cover or number of clumps to determine the extent of occupation and acres covered. For example, 21- by 21-foot plots represent 0.001 of an acre and can be evenly spaced across a stand of trees or area. Total the percent estimated cover or number of invasive stems counted per plot, divide these by the number of plots, and then multiple times 1,000 to gain an estimate of occupation for an average acre. An estimate for the entire area can be gained by multiplying the average times the number of acres in the surveyed area. By mapping the survey plot findings, areas of highest infestation density and multiple invasive species can be identified.

- *The third option is an inventory followed by monitoring.* Inventories are used to record the location and area of every infestation and the treatments that you apply. This is the best approach for individual land ownerships. Inventories can map individual patches and plants or circle them as a group when they occur in close proximity to one another. The GPS locations can be taken and mapped, or a sketch map made to plan the program of treatment and restoration. Monitoring requires revisits to inventoried points at scheduled times or resurveying tracks with scattered infestation to record and track treatment effectiveness and any further invasions.

- *The fourth option in the SSIMS method is surveillance.* A constant task for all those who work on and or otherwise use your land. Everyone should be alert for new infestations and know how to report these when and where sighted.

Handheld GPS Unit.

Surveyed GPS locations of invasive species.

Backpack GPS Unit.

4. Eradicate, control or contain, and monitor results. You can eradicate an infestation by eliminating every invasive plant and its seeds in the infestation, a difficult feat that requires timely and repeated use of the most effective treatments. You can control or suppress an infestation through medium effective treatments that mostly kill aboveground plant parts but that leave, even with repeated treatments, the live roots or rhizomes unharmed. You can contain an infestation by confining and restricting its spread through effective treatments that eliminate outlier plants, spots, or advancing fronts. Containment is often the only option when infestations continue to encroach from adjoining untreated lands. Remember: all treatments should be monitored for determining followup actions.

5. Rehabilitate, restore, or reclaim treated lands with resistant and resilient native or noninvasive plants. Critical to rehabilitating a site is promoting or planting desirable species that are as aggressive as the invasive species. Effective treatment schemes for rehabilitation use an integrated approach that combines treatments in an appropriate sequence and at crucial times.

Effective Treatments for Integrated Management of Nonnative Invasive Plants

A successful nonnative invasive plant management program usually involves a combination of treatment methods based on these and other available tools and resources:

1. **Herbicidal methods with selective and broadcast applications**
2. **Manual methods using hand tools**
3. **Mechanical methods using equipment**
4. **Cultural methods such as prescribed burning, water level control, planting, and seeding**
5. **Biological control methods that range from prescribed grazing to introduction of biological control agents such as insects and pathogens that feed solely on target weeds**
6. **Mulching and solarization methods**

Many methods are available to manage invasive plants and rehabilitate your site, and more are under development. A successful plan of attack depends on integrated management that considers all methods relative to the site and its invaders. These methods will be presented in greater detail.

Safety First

Safety is always a top priority when working in the difficult situations often presented by invasive plant infestations and treatments. As your first line of safety, use and maintain personal protective equipment (PPE) designed for a specific task. A task as seemingly simple as surveying a site requires PPE. The following are examples of PPE-based invasive plant management tasks:

Protect yourself with the right PPEs.

Suggested Personal Protective Equipment by Task
(herbicide applications must follow the label specified on the PPE's)

Task	Waterproof Boots	Hard Hat	Leather Gloves	Eye Protection	Safety Boots	Shin Guards	Hearing Protection	Neoprene Gloves	Appropriate Chaps
Surveying		X		X	X				
Mechanical Control			X	X	X				
Stem Injection		X	X	X	X			X	
Cut and Treat		X	X	X	X	X	X	X	X
Mixing Herbicides	X			X				X	X
Applying Herbicides				X				X	X
Girdling		X	X	X	X		X		

Required safety items for the field include a separate water container for washing, along with soap, paper towels, and trash bags as well as ample drinking water and a fully stocked first-aid kit.

Application of Herbicides

Adhere to the following precautions for safe application of herbicides:

- Take copies of all herbicide labels and material safety datasheets (MSDS) to the application site.
- An eyewash station is required for flushing accidentally splashed or sprayed herbicide from eyes.
- Take a change of clothes to the application site in case your clothes become contaminated and immediately wash off any herbicide spilled or sprayed on you.
- Always wash your hands and face thoroughly before eating, smoking, and when leaving the site.
- Always wash contaminated clothes and any clothing worn during spray applications separately from other garments.
- Adhere to any worker entry restrictions following treatment and worker notification requirements specified on the labels.

Transport of Herbicides

Adhere to the following precautions for safe transport of herbicides:

- Be sure containers are not damaged before loading or during transport.
- Take only the amount of herbicide, water, and adjuvants you need for the day.
- Do not transport herbicides in the passenger section of a vehicle.
- Do not transport herbicides in the trunk of passenger cars or in trucks with wooden beds. Use a trailer to transport herbicides when using a car.
- Secure all containers with ropes and straps to keep them from moving around. During the trip, check the containers periodically to be sure they have not shifted or spilled.
- At the application site, keep herbicide containers out of the sun. If you leave the containers in your vehicle, park in the shade. Place removed containers in shaded, cool areas. Direct sunlight can overheat herbicide containers and build pressure inside the containers. Use a tarp to shade exposed containers during transport and onsite storage.

Herbicide Spill Procedures

Follow these procedures for safely handling a spill:

- If an accident during transport results in a minor spill, administer first aid at once to anyone who may have been injured.
- Confine the spill by digging a dike around the spill area. Always take a shovel with you when hauling herbicides.
- Soak up the herbicide with an absorbent material, such as that used in automotive garages, or with clayey soil.
- Dispose of the contaminated absorbent as you would excess herbicide by spreading it on a treatment area unless local laws specify otherwise.

If a major spill occurs, follow the procedures given above and then call the manufacturer's helpline printed on the herbicide label. The manufacturer's helpline representative will tell you which authorities to notify and what further actions to take.

Remember to take to your application site a copy of the herbicide label and the MSDS provided to you at the time of purchase or found online by product name search. This is a State requirement. The herbicide label has many application details while the MSDS has more uniformly presented details, including the manufacturer's name; an emergency phone number; chemical ingredients in the formulation and their properties; health and fire fighting hazards; accident response measures; proper methods for handling, storage, transportation, and disposal; exposure controls and personal protection; and regulatory information. If an accident involves a person's physical exposure to a herbicide, the physician will need a copy of the MSDS.

Herbicide Application Methods

Most nonnative invasive plants in the South are perennials with extensive roots, tubers, or rhizomes. This means that effective herbicide applications offer the best means of containment or eradication, because herbicides can kill roots without baring soil—bared soil is susceptible to reinvasion and erosion. Decades of research has found that herbicides tested and registered with the U.S. Environmental Protection Agency (EPA) are safe to humans and other animals when stored, transported, and applied according to strict label directions. For successful herbicide treatments:

- Use the herbicide most effective for the targeted species and appropriate for safety to nontarget species and situation.
- Follow, in detail, the application methods prescribed on the label. Adhere to all label prohibitions, precautions, and safety requirements during herbicide transport, storage, mixing, and application.
- Choose the optimum time for applications. For foliar-applied herbicides to nonevergreen woody plants, the best time is usually midsummer to early fall and not later than a month before expected frost. Evergreens and semievergreens with leaves can be treated effectively in the winter. Optimum application times for many herbicides on invasive plants have not been fully researched and future findings should greatly assist to perfect prescriptions.
- Be patient. After application, herbicidal activity—detectable as yellowing of foliage or as leaves with dead spots or margins—may take a month or longer. Allow herbicides to work for several months to a year before resorting to other treatment options. Consult the herbicide label for timing of expected response of treated vegetation. But when green foliage reappears, retreatments should follow.

Selecting an Effective Herbicide

Herbicides registered by EPA for forestry use, wildlife openings, noncroplands, and fencerows in the Southern States will mainly be discussed here, although herbicides for other land use areas, such as rights-of-way, pastures, and rangelands, may be just as effective and may contain the same active ingredient. If a herbicide is not prohibited for use on a specific site, crop, or vegetation, then the broad category of noncrop areas even allows use in "nonused" lands and parks in urban and suburban environments. Some prescriptions for these other land types will also be given along with aquatic sites. Carefully read and study the herbicide label for information on specified areas of use, crops, and prohibitions. It is not necessary for the target invasive plant to be listed on the label for permitted use, except in specific States, like New Hampshire. There are a few State-specific prohibitions, such as Florida's prohibition of picloram herbicides, i.e., Tordon use.

Herbicides are identified by trade name and active ingredient name. Many active ingredients are now sold as generic herbicides at lower costs, while customer service and product liability may be different than the brand name products listed here.

Foliar-Active (Primarily) Herbicides

Enforcer® Brush Killer (triclopyr)
Glyphosate herbicides (glyphosate concentrations commonly range from 41 to 54 percent) such as:
    Accord® Concentrate
    Glyphomax® Plus
    Roundup® Original
    Roundup Pro® Concentrate
    Rodeo® (aquatic)
Garlon® 3A (triclopyr)
Garlon® 4 (triclopyr ester)
Garlon® 4 Ultra (triclopyr ester)
Krenite® S (fosamine)
ORTHO® Brush-B-Gon® (triclopyr)
Pathfinder® II (triclopyr in oil)
Renovate® 3 (aquatic triclopyr)
Vista® XRT (fluroxypyr)

Foliar and Soil-Active Herbicides

Arsenal® AC (imazapyr)
Arsenal® PowerLine™ (imazapyr)
Chopper® Gen2 (imazapyr)
Clearcast® (imazamox aquatic)
Escort® XP (metsulfuron)
Habitat® (imazapyr aquatic)
Hyvar® X-L (bromacil)
Journey® (imazapic + glyphosate)
Milestone® VM (aminopyralid)
Outrider® (sulfosulfuron)
Overdrive® (diflufenzopyr + dicamba)
Pathway® (2,4-D + picloram)
Plateau® (imazapic)
Tordon® 101 (2,4-D + picloram, Restricted use)
Tordon® K (picloram, Restricted use)
Tordon® RTU (2,4-D + picloram)
Transline® (clopyralid)
Stalker® (imazapyr)
Vanquish® (dicamba)
Velpar L® (hexazinone)

Because nonnative invasive plants are usually difficult to control, selecting the most effective herbicide(s) is important. Often herbicides that have both soil and foliar activity are most effective with the least number of applications. However, applying herbicides with soil activity can damage desirable plants when their roots are present in the treatment zone or when herbicides move downslope to untreated areas following heavy rainfall. Garlon herbicides are mainly foliar active, but they have some soil activity at high rates or when mixed with oils. Garlon 4 and Vanquish can volatilize or vaporize at high temperatures, and their residues can move by air currents to affect surrounding plants; therefore, avoid application of these herbicides on days when temperatures exceed 80 °F. Avoid applications when rainfall is anticipated, unless soil activation is needed. Consult the label for the rainfast period. Delay applications during severe drought because herbicides are not as effective when plants go into stress dormancy during dry periods.

When possible, use selective herbicides that target specific nonnative species, e.g., Transline, which controls mainly legumes and composites and minimizes damage to surrounding desirable plants even though they receive herbicide contact. Minimizing damage to desirable plants also can be achieved by making applications when they are dormant. For example, apply basal sprays to the bark of invasives in late winter before most other plants emerge, or foliar spray evergreen or semievergreen invasives after surrounding plants have entered dormancy. Remember that desirable woody plants can be damaged through transfer of herbicides by root exudates following stem injection and cut-treat treatments or when soil-active herbicides wash off treated stems. Damage to surrounding native plants can be minimized with care and forethought during planning and application.

Adjuvants and Additives to Herbicide Spray Solutions

Adjuvants are any product other than water added to a spray solution to improve herbicide performance and effectiveness, including delivery, retention on foliage, and foliar or bark penetration. Adjuvants may be included as part of the commercial herbicide product or sold separately as an additive you must mix with the herbicide before application. Another common additive used by professionals is a marking dye, which is not an adjuvant. Choose an adjuvant according to label recommendations and appropriate for your particular application method and field conditions. Be aware that many adjuvants are sold under invalid claims and unproven results. Before purchasing an adjuvant, ask for recommendations from reliable, certified distributors, applicators, or extension specialists. Useful adjuvants and additives include the following and are classified here according to their type of action.

Marking dyes and colorants, used in selective or broadcast herbicide applications, verify that the treatment was applied to the intended target. Application dyes show how well target vegetation has been covered and whether harmful contact has been made with nontarget vegetation or with the applicator. Although dyes are messy and short-lived as visible markers, they are helpful in training applicators and checking the quality of applications. Common dyes include Bullseye® Blue Spray Pattern Indicator, Hi-Light® Blue Indicator, and Blazon® Blue Spray Pattern Indicator. Bullseye is a water-soluble polymeric colorant, not a dye, and nonstaining on skin, clothing, and equipment. Bas-Oil® Red is oil-soluble and used with basal oil mixes.

Spray colorant indicates coverage.

Surface active agents (better known by the acronym *surfactants*) are a broad group of materials that facilitate the emulsifying, dispersing, spreading, wetting, and other surface modifying properties of liquids. Surfactants increase herbicide activity by making droplets larger on the leaf, thus improving penetration of the plant. Herbicide, weed species, and environmental conditions affect surfactant performance. Surfactants should be used with most foliar applications, except when prohibited by the herbicide label for specific uses, such as safety to desirable seeds and seedlings. Nonionic surfactants are usually recommended because they enhance wetting and retention of spray drops and do not bind with the herbicide molecule to cause deactivation. Never use household detergents as surfactants because they can deactivate many herbicides. Common surfactants include Entry II®, Big Sur 90, and Timbersurf 90. A newer type of surfactant with leaf penetrating action and rainfastness is based on organosilicones, with commonly used products being Sil Energy® and Silwet® L-77. These must be mixed exactly or they will be ineffective. They also increase the risk of injury to skin and eyes during application. Organosilicones are now commonly blended with other surfactants for additive properties.

Water conditioners are spray solution additives that enhance herbicide performance by preventing deactivation of the herbicide's active ingredient. Ammoniated salts are added to prevent loss of herbicidal activity of glyphosate and picloram when using "hard water" with greater than 200 parts per million of calcium, magnesium, and potassium. Acidifiers and buffers are additives sometimes listed on herbicide labels for use with specific water sources. Ammoniated salts, buffers, and surfactants are now blended to combine their activities in special spray additives. Common water conditioners are Choice® Weather Master, and AMSWC™ (just ammonium sulfate). Because dirt and organic debris can cause herbicide deactivation, always mix herbicides only with clean water from a filtered and treated source.

Vegetable oils, such as methylated seed oil (MSO), can increase spray drop adherence to leaves, increase herbicide penetration of leaves, and slow evaporation during and after application. Herbicides must remain in solution on a leaf for plant uptake. Vegetable oils also are mixed in basal sprays, and some vegetable oils contain emulsifying agents for this purpose. Several new formulations of herbicides come with vegetable oils. Common MSOs are Improved JLB Oil Plus and DYNE-AMIC®. A commonly used bark oil is Aqumix®.

Drift retardants thicken spray solutions to create larger drops that are less likely to drift in wind, permitting more accurate applications in light wind and continued applications in slightly windier conditions. Common drift retardants are Poly Control 2, Nalcotrol®, and Sta-Put® Deposition Aid.

Penetrants partially dissolve waxy plant surfaces to help the herbicide penetrate leaves or move through bark. Common penetrants are Cide-Kick® and Cide-Kick® II.

Defoamers dissolve foam in spray tanks to improve mixing and transfers of herbicides like Arsenal AC and Velpar® L. Common defoamers are Fighter-F®10, Foam Fighter®, and Brewer's Defoamer.

Mixing Herbicides

Always use clean water in herbicide spray solutions. Thoroughly mix all ingredients before applications. Unevenly mixed herbicide solutions will produce uneven results. For large batch mixing of 5 to 200 gallons, the mixing or application tank must have an agitation system and must be operated for a sufficient time to produce a uniform mix.

Never mix herbicides in a backpack sprayer because their shape inhibits thorough mixing. Instead, always mix herbicide sprays for backpack sprayers in a separate mixing container to a point that guarantees uniformity. Mix individual batches with a stirrer in a bucket. For large batches, fill backpack sprayers from a mixing tank that has an agitation system. Fill the mixing bucket or mixing tank one-half to three-quarters full with clean water. Add herbicides at label-recommended rates, with carefully calculated and measured amounts of ingredients, stirring or agitating the mixture as you add these. For best results, add herbicide types, additives, and adjuvants in the following order: (1) water conditioners and defoamers, (2) dry flowables (like Escort XP), (3) emulsifiable concentrates (like Garlon 4), (4) water-soluble liquids (like glyphosate herbicides), (5) most adjuvants, and (6) drift retardants. Over time, dry flowables and other herbicides, along with oil additives, can settle to the bottom of a tank and must be periodically agitated as specified on the label.

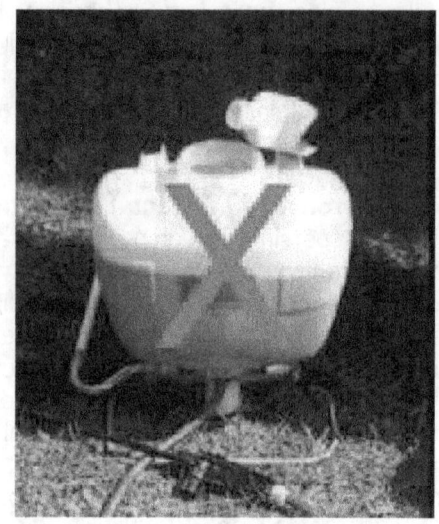

Do not mix in a sprayer.

Do mix in a bucket with a stirrer.

Backpack Sprayers

Backpack sprayers vary greatly in design and capabilities, and many versions are available commercially. The most desirable components of a backpack sprayer are a streamlined shape (to make it easy for the applicator to move through dense vegetation), an impact-resistant tank equipped with a large opening (for filling), and a solid screen (to trap debris).

All backpack sprayers and spray guns should have chemical-resistant seals. Viton® seals are made of the most durable materials and allow handling of both oil- and water-based mixtures. Backpacks with internal pressure regulators can help the applicator ensure uniform rates of application and minimize drift that otherwise might result from using too much pressure. Some models feature kink-resistant hoses for improved safety and reliability. Comfort and support in the design of a backpack sprayer cannot be overstated. Padded shoulder straps with harnesses that attach securely to the frame can reduce operator fatigue and accidents, especially in dense vegetation or on uneven terrain.

Models of backpack sprayers.

Steven T. Manning

Backpack sprayers come with a piston or diaphragm pump. Piston pumps must have a regulator because they generate higher pressures. An added pressure gauge on the wand handle can help the applicator maintain a spray pressure appropriate for the given treatment. Another useful addition to a backpack sprayer is a more durable metal spray wand with a more precise shutoff valve than the valve on a flexible plastic wand. Quality backpack sprayers, which are preferred by commercial applicators, usually come with a 1- to 3-year warranty.

Spray Nozzles

Choosing the best nozzle will usually require that you purchase another nozzle and not use the one that comes with your sprayer. Correct nozzles can greatly improve effectiveness and efficiency. Nozzles consist of a nozzle body, a cap, and a tip with the orifice. The spray tip is the most important part of your sprayer because it breaks the liquid into droplets of the correct size and forms the spray pattern.

Tips are made of a variety of materials. Most readily available tips are made of plastic, brass, and stainless steel. Tips of harder materials initially may cost more but will pay for themselves in the long run with durability and consistent performance. Plastic tips tend to have very irregular spray patterns. Brass tips can be easily damaged during cleaning, and such damage will cause irregular spray patterns. It is a good practice to discard plastic or brass nozzles that come standard with a sprayer and replace them with tips of stainless steel designed for long-term commercial use. Stainless steel tips provide a uniform and consistent spray pattern over longer periods and are known for having fewer out-of-the-box defects.

Air induction tips are newer modifications. These tips produce large, air-filled drops that help reduce the potential for drift in winds. They work by drawing air through two holes in the nozzle sides, which blends the air with the herbicide mix. They emit a spray of large droplets filled with air bubbles and virtually no drift-prone droplets. Other nozzle alternatives include "low-drift" and "extended-range" tips that produce fewer small stray droplets and aerosols that contribute to drift compared to conventional nozzles. When choosing air induction or stainless steel nozzles, consider models with a plastic body and a steel tip, because these models are as durable as more expensive all-steel nozzles.

Low-volume directed sprays are often applied with a backpack sprayer and a spray wand equipped with a full cone, flat-fan, or adjustable cone spray tip. The tip has the orifice, which is usually identified by a four-digit number representing its spray pattern angle and flow-volume specifications; for example, an 8002 tip has a spray pattern angle of 80 degrees and a flow volume of 0.2 gallons per minute (all flow volumes are measured at 40 pounds per square inch of pressure). When your application is for invasive plants, models SS4004E (SS = stainless steel, E = even pattern); SS8004E; SS2504; and a wide-angle flooding nozzle like the Floodjet TK VS3 yield good coverage, useful flow rates, and are good additions to your toolkit.

Nozzle spray angles of 65 and 120 degrees.

Even flat fan spray tip — SS4004E.

A range of tips should be carried to the field so that the best nozzle for plant heights, terrain, and weather can be selected. To purchase nozzles and spray components and parts, consult an agricultural products outlet, farm tractor dealer, or farm store. Major sources are Spraying Systems Company (630–665–5000, www.spray.com, info@spray.com); Dultmeier Sales (888–677–5054, www.dultmeier.com/div_agricultural.asp, dultmeier@dultmeier.com); and Forestry Suppliers Inc. (800–752–8460, www.forestry-suppliers.com, www.forestry-suppliers.com/c01_pages/contact.asp). These few are provided to assist the reader, while there are other manufacturers and distributors.

Flooding nozzle.

Flooding nozzle spray pattern.

Sprayer Preparation

Prior to calibration of equipment and application of herbicides, applicators must properly prepare their equipment. Thoroughly clean all nozzles, screens, and filters in detergent solution, using a soft bristle brush, and then rinse. Make certain that all nozzles are the same size, prescribed for the application, and made of the same material for uniformity by all applicators and especially when several nozzles are along a short boom. Replace nozzles that do not have uniform spray patterns (often determined by spraying along a concrete surface). Check flow rates periodically by catching spray in a container over a timed period. Stay alert for dripping nozzles and use check values to prevent drips. Select an operating pressure consistent with the desired gallons per acre output and spray pattern relative to wind conditions. Check all PPE, replace faulty items, and make certain that all applicators are trained in use and maintenance of all items. Always use the appropriate PPE for each operation, and perform daily maintenance on this equipment.

Backpack Sprayer Calibration

Prescriptions for invasive plant applications are often given as percent-solutions of specific herbicides. But on herbicide labels, most prescriptions are given in herbicide volume or weight (dry herbicides) per acre. This requires calibration of a spray system using the same nozzle(s) and pressure that will be used during application. Calibration is simply the determination of how much spray volume is applied to a specified area of land. Calibration requires timing an application to a known area, which is then expressed as gallons per acre. This should be done in the treatment area because factoring in the speed of the applicator who works in those conditions is crucial for accurate calibration. Water alone should be used for calibration procedure.

- For calibrating broadcast sprays, measure the width of the spray swath in feet and multiply this measurement by the distance traveled in feet for 1 minute. Convert this result to an acre basis by dividing the square feet by 43,560 square feet per acre.
- Catch the spray from the nozzle(s) for 1 minute and measure the volume in ounces. Convert this measurement to gallons by dividing by 128 ounces per gallon.
- Gallons per acre then can be calculated by dividing the measured gallons by the part of an acre treated.

The calculated "gallons per acre" output during application will be a mixture of herbicide, water, and any additional adjuvants. The amount of herbicide prescribed per acre is specified on the label or in this book; this is the amount you should mix with the "gallons per acre" determined during calibration. For example, if a prescription calls for 2 gallons of herbicide per acre, and if your sprayer is calibrated to apply 20 gallons per acre, then, to treat 1 acre, you must mix 2 gallons of herbicide in 18 gallons of water and adjuvants. For mixing an individual batch for a 4-gallon backpack sprayer, you would divide these quantities by 5. If you need to apply more or less gallons per acre as specified on the label or dictated by vegetation conditions, the nozzle size(s) and/or pressure should be changed. Higher pressures or larger tips will increase output, while increasing pressure may increase drift potential.

You can use the same calculation methods for foliar-directed sprays and for sprayers mounted on tractors and other equipment. For foliar sprays, you will treat individual plants in the measured area (some part of an acre) and then you can refill your sprayer according to a marked pre-application level to determine the gallons applied. For calculations of mounted sprayers, you will need to consider a large calibration area and capture spray from all nozzles, both over a timed period as before.

Selective Herbicide Applications

Although treating extensive infestations may require broadcast treatments of herbicide sprays or pellets by helicopter or tractor-mounted application systems, the best approach is usually selective applications to target nonnative plants while avoiding or minimizing application to desirable plants. The selective methods described below are directed foliar sprays and wipes, basal sprays and wipes, stem injection, cut-treat, basal sprays, and soil spots.

Directed Foliar Sprays and Wipes

Directed foliar sprays are herbicide-water-adjuvant solutions aimed at target plant foliage to wet all leaves, applied by either low- or high-volume sprayers. Herbicide application by directed foliar spray is one of the most cost-effective methods for treating many types of herbaceous and woody invasive plant species. With this method, herbicide mixtures are applied to the foliage and especially the growing tips of woody plants, or to completely cover herbaceous plants. Foliar sprays can be applied whenever leaves are present but, for woody plant control, are usually most effective from midsummer to late fall. Winter and spring applications are also effective in controlling specific species and are often required to prevent seed formation.

Spray shield from a used gallon milk jug (bottom removed and cap bored).

Selective treatment is possible because the applicator can direct the spray towards target plants and away from desirable plants. The addition of a spray shield to the end of the wand confines spray to the target. Another safeguard is to only use foliar-active herbicides, because directed sprays of soil-active herbicides can damage or kill surrounding plants when their roots are within the treatment zone. Never use herbicides with soil activity to treat invasive plants under desirable trees or shrubs that are susceptible to the herbicide. If nontarget foliage is accidently sprayed, clip off the foliage to prevent uptake.

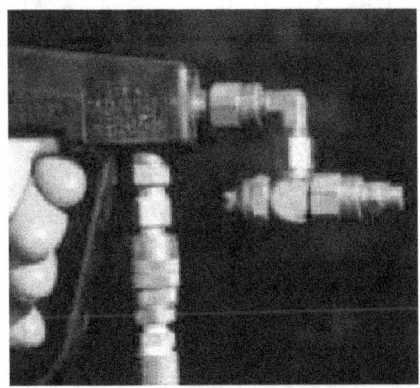
Spray gun with rollover valve that holds two tips.

Low-volume foliar sprays using spray tips and spraying pressures of 20 to 30 pounds per square inch can ensure productivity and limit drift to surrounding plants. Plants up to 6 feet tall can be treated with this equipment, while the addition of a commercially available wand extension can slightly increase height capabilities. To treat plants up to about 18 feet tall, use higher spray pressures with a straight-stream or narrow flat-fan tip. Wind must be minimal (less than 2 miles per hour) and used by the applicator to facilitate upper crown coverage. A handgun with a rollover valve can replace the spray wand and accommodates two tips, such as a flat fan for close spraying and a narrow flat fan or adjustable cone nozzle for tall plant spraying. This setup greatly extends applicator capabilities and productivity when invasive infestations vary in height. Sturdy metal wands can replace plastic ones for more precise applications. Small booms with multiple nozzles can replace the single-nozzle wand for better productivity and efficiency in treating large areas of low-growing invasives.

Directed foliar sprays can be applied in higher volumes by using spray wands attached by hoses to vehicle-mounted spraying systems that have much larger herbicide tank capacities. The high-volume directed foliar spray is the most efficient approach to large infestations of multiple invasive species where there are few nontarget plants.

Directed spraying kudzu from a bucket-truck.

Dennis Markwardt

High-volume directed sprays.

Steven T. Manning

Handheld weed wicks and rollers apply ultra-low volumes by wiping the herbicide mix onto the target leaf surfaces or bark; the herbicide mixture is contained in the handle. A few commercial models are manufactured in Australia and New Zealand, but devices also can be handmade from PVC tubing, fittings, and a sealed on sponge or rope wick and fitted to the wand of a backpack sprayer. Most wick systems have limited use and durability in forest and field situations, but are useful when the applicator needs to avoid applying herbicide to rare or protected plants. Similar to a weed wick applicator, a roll-

Foliar wick applicator.

ing sponge head is another drift-free tool option that allows application directly to targeted species.

The THINVERT Application System uses a series of special spray nozzles to apply thin invert emulsion spray solutions (thin mayonnaise-like consistency) to greatly reduce drift and evaporation of spray particles on the plant surface. The nozzles and

Handmade basal bark wiper.

a combination of special oil soluble herbicide (triclopyr) and emulsifying agent have been developed and sold by Arborchem Products Company (717–766–6661, www.arborchem.com). This system combines the unique spray nozzle and spray carrier into a coordinated unit for aerial or ground applications to roadsides, rangeland, cropland, industrial sites, forests, and landscape areas. Thinvert sprays can be applied to foliage as well as stems or cut-stumps where absolutely no drift can be tolerated, such as immediately adjacent to neighboring croplands and special rare plant habitats.

THINVERT Application System.

Basal Sprays and Wipes

Basal sprays are herbicide-oil-penetrant mixtures sprayed on the lower portion of woody shrub, vine, and tree stems. The sprays are usually applied with a backpack sprayer or wick applicator. Basal sprays are best where most trees are less than 8 inches diameter breast height (d.b.h.), but can be used on much larger trees of susceptible species. Application is to smooth juvenile bark by thoroughly wetting the lower 12 to 20 inches of the trunk, up to 36 inches on larger trees to the groundline including the root-collar area and any exposed roots. Smaller trees and shrubs are controlled with less coverage. Avoid spray contact with desirable trees or heavy use within their root zone.

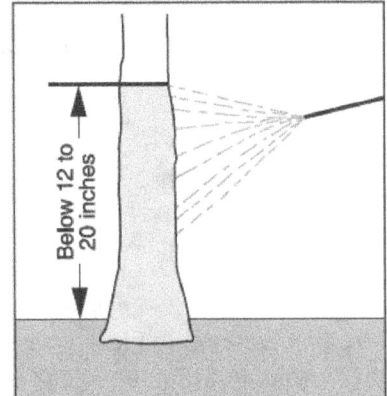

Basal spray applications.

The herbicide must be an oil-soluble ester formulation, such as Garlon 4 and Stalker, and mixed with a special basal oil product, penetrating oil, diesel fuel, fuel oil, mineral oil, vegetable oil with a penetrant, or blends of these ingredients. Appropriate oils will be specified on the label. Some oils may be prohibited for application in riparian areas and wetlands. Use an adjustable cone nozzle with a coarse spray. For less off-target spray on smaller trees, use an even flat-fan nozzle with a fairly narrow angle and low volume (such as a 4002E, oriented crosswise to the wand for a spray that lands in a vertical band on the stem).

Pathfinder II is sold ready to use as a mixture of triclopyr ester herbicide mixed with oil in the container.

Spray dye for basal spray.

A modified method, streamlined basal sprays, is effective for many woody species up to 2 inches in groundline diameter and susceptible species up to 6 inches in diameter, such as privets. Equipment for this treatment is a backpack sprayer with a spray gun and a low-flow straight-stream or narrow-angle spray tip. To prevent waste, maintain pressure below 30 pounds per square inch with a pressure regulator. At this pressure, an effective reach of 9 feet is possible while bark splash is minimized. For treating stems less than 2 inches in diameter, apply the stream of spray up and down single stems for about 6 to 8 inches or apply across multiple stems in 2- to 3-inch-wide bands. This multiple-band treatment also can be effective on larger stems. Direct the spray stream to smooth juvenile bark about 4 to 18 inches from the ground and below branches. Stems that are thick barked or near 3 inches in diameter require treatment on all sides.

The most effective time period in most of the South for a basal spray and streamline is June through September, while winter treatments are easier when leaves do not block access and spray. Fall, winter, and late spring applications are often not as effective, though the period from February 15 to April 1 has shown acceptable results. After treating with a basal spray, wait at least 6 months before cutting dead trees, because herbicide activity within plant roots can continue for an extended period.

Streamline basal spray.

24

Stem Injection

Stem injection (including hack-and-squirt) involves herbicide concentrate or herbicide-water mixtures applied into downward incision cuts spaced around woody stems. Cuts are made by an ax, hatchet, machete, brush ax, cane knife, or a variety of cutting tools and even cordless drills. Tree injection is a selective method of controlling larger trees, shrubs, and vines (greater than 2 inches in d.b.h.) with minimum damage to surrounding plants. Stem injection is the fastest and most cost-effective method for nonnative trees and large shrubs. Injection treatments are sometimes not as effective in controlling multiple-stemmed species compared to the faster basal bark treatments, but may be easier in remote or rough terrain where a backpack sprayer might be impractical or cumbersome. Stem injection is physically demanding for the applicator, who must repeatedly and accurately strike target trees with a sharp tool before delivering the herbicide into the cut. For best results, sharpen tools frequently.

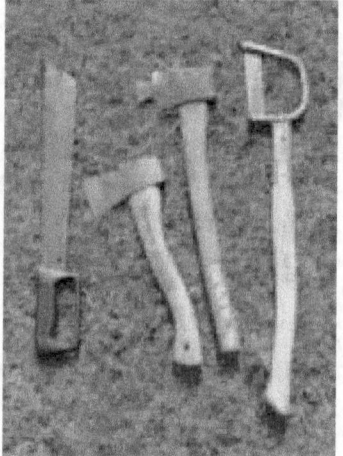

Cutting tools for hack-and-squirt treatment.

Cane knife.

Incisions must be deep enough to penetrate the bark and inner bark, slightly into the wood. Do not make multiple cuts directly above or below each other because this will inhibit movement of the herbicide within the stem. A complete girdle or frill of the stem is not needed or desirable. Space the injection cuts 1 to 1.5 inches apart edge to edge (or per label instructions) around the circumference of each trunk individually or within a clump at a convenient height. Use a handheld, chemical-resistant 1- to 2-quart spray bottle to apply 0.5 to 2 mL of concentrated herbicide or dilutions (prescribed on the label) into the cut. The amount will depend on the size of cut and how much the cut can hold without the herbicide running onto the bark. Apply herbicide to each cut until the exposed area is thoroughly wet. The herbicide should remain in the injection cut to avoid wasting herbicide and to prevent damage of surrounding plants. All injected herbicides can reach untreated plants by root grafts between like species, and uptake of root exudates by all species results in nontarget damage. Herbicides with soil activity can damage nearby plants when washed from incisions into the soil by unexpected rainfall soon after application. Avoid injection treatments if rainfall is predicted within 48 hours.

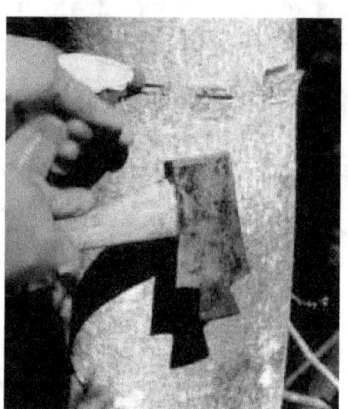

Hack-and-squirt method.

Penetrate the bark and inner bark, slightly into the wood.

Steven T. Manning

Apply herbicide into each cut until thoroughly wet.

Steven T. Manning

Special tree injectors are available that combine the cutting operation with automated herbicide delivery. For injecting some herbicides (amine formulations), the Hypo-Hatchet® Tree injector (Forestry Suppliers Inc., 800–647–5368, www.forestry-suppliers.com) consists of a steel hatchet connected to a herbicide container (worn on belt) by tubing. The injector delivers a set amount of herbicide into the cut. Daily cleaning and lubrication of the impact piston is required maintenance, along with periodic replacement of rubber o-rings and seals. Check all hoses and fittings before use for leaks and make appropriate repairs to prevent accidental exposure of herbicide to the applicator. When working with the Hypo-Hatchet in dense infestations, be mindful of the supply tubing, which might become tangled and easily disconnected.

Hypo Hatchet® Tree Injector.

Another injector is the EZ-Ject®, which consists of a steel lance that holds 400 shells of glyphosate or imazapyr herbicides (ArborSystems, 888–395–6732, www.ezject.com). The head of the lance is placed against the base of the target woody plant, and a manual thrust jams the shell through the bark into the inner bark. As with other injection methods, these shells are spaced around each stem. The EZ-Ject is the most efficient and effective injection option for treating multi-stemmed, low-branching shrubs like privets, silverthorn (*Elaeagnus pungens* Thunb.), and bush honeysuckles (*Lonicera* spp.), as well as large entangled vines like oriental bittersweet (*Celastrus orbiculatus* Thunb.). Shell jamming has been reported as a problem when using the EZ-Ject to treat extensive infestations. Removing the herbicide shells when not in use, proper use, and daily maintenance can help prevent jamming.

EZ-Ject® tree injector.

Tree injection can be applied at most times throughout the year, but December to the middle of January seems to be least effective in the Midsouth. Prolonged cold temperatures can freeze herbicide in the cut, resulting in poor absorption. Heavy spring sapflow can wash herbicide from incision cuts, resulting in poor control and soil transfer to nontarget plants. Prolonged and severe drought is also an ineffective period.

Cut-Treat

Cut-treat involves applying herbicide concentrates, herbicide-water or herbicide-penetrant mixtures to the outer circumference of freshly cut stumps or the entire top surface of cut stems. Applications are made with a spray bottle, backpack sprayer, wick, or paint brush. Freshly cut stems and stumps of trees, woody vines, shrubs, canes, and bamboo stems can be treated with herbicide mixtures to prevent resprouting and to kill roots. It is critical that the cut is made as low as possible to the ground, and that the stem is treated immediately after the cut is made. Invasives not treated with herbicides after cutting invariably resprout and intensify their infestation. Cutting is usually by chainsaw or brush saw but can be made by handsaws and cutting blades.

Cut-treat the circumference of large stems, and the entire top of small stems.

A 2-quart pressured spray bottle works well for stump treatment.

Cut stems low for treating.

To minimize deactivation of the herbicide in the cut-treat method, remove sawdust from stumps before treatment. For stumps over 3 inches in diameter, completely wet the outer edge with the herbicide or herbicide mixture. Make certain that the solution thoroughly covers the wood next to the bark of the stump. Completely wet the tops of smaller stumps and all cut stems in a clump. Apply a basal spray mixture of herbicide, oil, and penetrant to stumps that have gone untreated for over 2 hours. Make certain to wet stump sides and root collar to further prevent sprouting.

The most effective time for the cut-treat method has not been determined for all invasive species, while summer and fall have shown to provide good control. One-year research results show that spring cut-treat with Garlon 4 on large Chinese privet is completely effective. Although winter treatments are slightly less effective than growing season applications, the absence of foliage on some cut stems and branches produces some offsetting gains in application efficiency.

Hand Sprayers for Injection and Cut-Treat

Most commercial hand sprayers are for occasional weekend household use. If you require a model for heavier duty and continuous daily operations, consider a sprayer with chemical-resistant Viton seals and a manual handpump. A good hand sprayer also will have an adjustable mist nozzle and a large filling opening. Models with a pump compression design are good for cutting and treating, while trigger-action pumps are better suited for stem injection or soil spot treatments. A full-grip valve will prevent fingertip fatigue with prolonged daily use of finger trigger valves.

Household use sprayer.

Handsaws or Cutting Blades

Chainsaws

A chainsaw with a 12- to 14-inch bar is best for felling most woody invasive plants since they are light weight and suited for cutting multiple stems in clumps. Professional tree saws are usually the lightest on the market and the tool of choice among contractors.

Brush Saws

Brush saws are large gasoline-powered weed eaters with a circular saw blade for cutting woody stems. While many large and expensive brush clearing saws are on the market, the high-end professional model is the preference of contractors for large projects. Special chainsaw-like tooth blades around a disc are the most efficient for cutting invasive plants and can be sharpened in the field throughout the life of the blade.

Brushsaw clears small stems.

Brushsaw blade with chainsaw-like teeth.

Small chainsaw for cutting.

Soil Spots

Spots of soil-active herbicides (mainly Velpar L and Hyvar X-L) are applied as spaced metered amounts around target woody stems or in a grid pattern for treating many stems in an area. Spots are usually applied with a utility spray bottle (herbicide-resistant seals preferred) or with operator-timed pulses from a hand sprayer or backpack sprayer equipped with a straight-stream nozzle. This method requires attention to preparing exact amounts and making prescribed spacings in strict accordance with specifications on herbicide labels or label supplements. It is effective only on specific nonnative plant species and usually only in spring and early summer. Any desirable plant with roots in the spot area can be killed or injured, making this appropriate only for dense infestations of a single invasive species such as tallowtree [*Triadica sebifera* (L.) Small], bamboos (*Phyllostachys* spp. and *Bambusa* spp.), and Brazilian peppertree (*Schinus terebinthifoliu* Raddi). Loblolly pine (*Pinus taeda* L.) is tolerant to Velpar L, and, thus, can be released from susceptible invasive shrubs and trees.

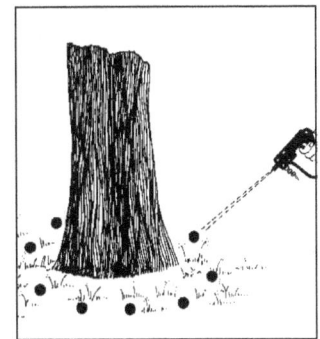

Basal soil spots.

Under Development: Pneumatic Applicator for Herbicide Ballistic Technology

New equipment options under development for invasive plant management include paintball guns with herbicide-filled ammunition for basal applications. Researchers at the University of Hawaii are studying how paintball guns might help selectively control a variety of species in hard-to-reach areas. From the ground or helicopter, sharpshooters can apply herbicides in a very selective manner with this tool.

Paintball gun basal application of herbicides.

Basal hit with herbicide-filled paintball.

Broadcast Herbicide Applications

Many infestations of nonnative plants are too extensive or dense to permit selective herbicide applications, and instead require broadcast methods. Herbicides with appropriate selectivity can be used to minimize damage when native species are tolerant. Broadcast applications can be discontinued in pockets of nontarget native plants, where selective methods are more appropriate. In special plant habitats, small desirable plants can be protected by plastic covers during broadcast treatment. Broadcast sprays of herbicides without soil activity can be applied to evergreen or early greening invasives when native plants are dormant. Many equipment types are available for mounting broadcast application systems suitable for the situation.

Utility Skid and Trailer-Mounted Sprayers

Complete spray systems are available mounted on utility skids for hauling in truck beds and as trailers for towing behind many types of equipment. Sprayers for treating invasives often have a tank with 100- to 250-gallon capacity and require 100- to 200-foot hose reels attached to a handgun. A variety of handguns and nozzles allow applicators to adjust spray volume, distance, and pattern. Sprayer pumps are usually powered by 2-stroke gasoline engines that require availability of adequate fuel and oil onsite. Truck- and trailer-mounted sprayers are parked at a convenient location, from where the applicator walks with a sprayer handgun into the infestation. The chief benefit of mounted sprayers is their capacity for holding and applying high volumes of herbicide-water mixtures. But their benefit is checked by such limitations as accessibility to the infestation, hose length and weight, and provisioning of water in the field. Of mounted sprayers, the skid steer-mounted sprayer is best for getting into difficult terrain and stands.

Machine mountable sprayer.

Basic Spraying Systems

Basic spraying systems for broadcast treatments have the following components: (1) tank, (2) pump, (3) strainer, (4) pressure regulator, (5) pressure gauge, (6) off and on valve, and (7) nozzle(s). Additional off and on valves are placed at convenient locations and additional strainers to protect components from undue wear. The spray tank should be equipped with an agitation system, or spray ingredients can be mixed in a separate mixing tank. For extended field operations, the system must include an additional water-supply tank equipped with a pump or gravity dispensing device.

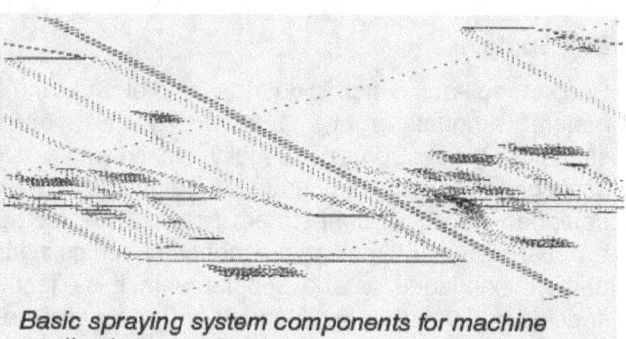

Basic spraying system components for machine applications.

All-Terrain Vehicle and Recreational-Type Vehicle Mounted Sprayers

ATV sprayers are best for selective applications in sensitive areas. Newly designed sprayers can hold 16, 24, or 40 gallons with optional front tank add-ons for many ATV models. Models have boom and/or boomless nozzles for broadcast application and a hose with spray gun for spot treatments. Recreational-type vehicles (RTVs) or Gators are larger than ATVs and carry a larger amount of herbicide mixture, with a capacity of up to 150 gallons. RTVs are a better option than ATVs for spraying rights-of-way and larger swaths of herbaceous plants, because the wide turn radius of RTVs makes them unsuitable for narrow areas. ATVs, with a tighter turn radius, are suited for repeated back-and-forth narrow swaths.

RTV mounted sprayer with Boom-Buster nozzles.

ATV mounted sprayer with front and rear tanks.

ATV mounted sprayer with a boom.

Tractor-Mounted Sprayers

Spray systems can be mounted on farm tractors, four-wheel drive tractors, skidders, forwarders, and crawler tractors. Tractor-mounted sprayers are useful for large prairie and forest restorations as well as right-of-way projects. Interchangeable attachments allow the operator to use the tractor for herbicide application as well as for many other attachments such as seed

Tractor sprayer with long boom for prairie restoration.

drills. Tractor-mounted tanks have a capacity of 200 to 600 gallons of spray solution per tank, supporting a much larger workload than other ground equipment. Tractors have an assortment of implements that can be used not only for spraying for invasive plant control, but disking and seeding for restoration as well.

Boom Jet® nozzle on a crawler tractor spraying kudzu.

Spray nozzle systems for tractors are usually boomless, which means the spray streams are projected from the tractor. There are several boomless nozzle systems that range greatly in price and in control of spray pattern and droplet size.

The following is a list of boomless nozzle systems ranging from cheapest (with the most variable pattern and droplet control) to most expensive (with the most precise pattern and droplet control):

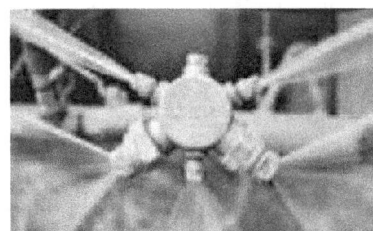

5880 Boom Jet® is a traditional, rugged, and inexpensive system. It consists of a cluster of five spray tips mounted on a circular head. Nozzles can be changed to match needs. Producing a very non-uniform spray pattern and range of droplet sizes, it is useful for treating shrubby invasives when an elevated mounting can gain spray height above the canopy.

Spraying Systems Inc., 5880 Boom Jet® nozzle with five tips.

The Boom Buster Nozzle is an elongated off-center nozzle of stainless steel with a gaping orifice opening from the end and running along the lower side. A nylon diffuser blade is positioned in the end of the orifice where a "hard edge" is formed for long-distance ejection of the spray solution. By mounting one or two nozzles perpendicular to the direction of tractor travel, the broad spray fans are directed to the side and behind the spray vehicle.

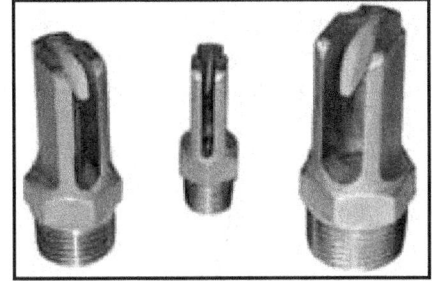

Boom Buster nozzles.

Spray pattern of two Boom Buster nozzles.

Boominator® Spray Nozzle is a circular machined stainless steel nozzle designed for left or right mounting. This configuration extends side reach and provides a wide spray pattern with approximately 15 degrees kickback under the nozzle for coverage immediately behind the tractor.

Boominator® spray nozzle sizes.

The Radiarc® Sprayer is a controlled droplet application system that produces droplets of uniform size. It uses direct electric power with rheostat adjustments to oscillate, in opposite directions, 2 circular heads of 11 tips each. It combines spray pressure (about 40 pounds per square inch) and centrifugal force to produce uniform droplets of large diameter for minimal drift. The 22 tips are evenly spaced around half the circular heads, producing semicircles of radiating spray that merge through oscillation behind and to the sides of the tractor. Spray pattern versatility is provided by a range of spray tip sizes. The system provides uniform pattern and droplet size, and can be elevated mounted where necessary to gain treatment height.

Boominator® spray pattern.

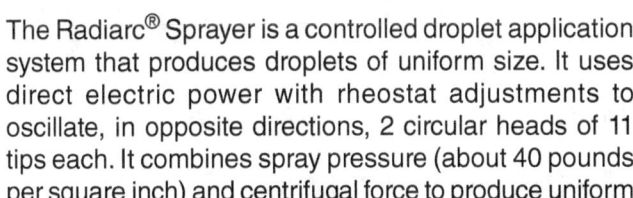

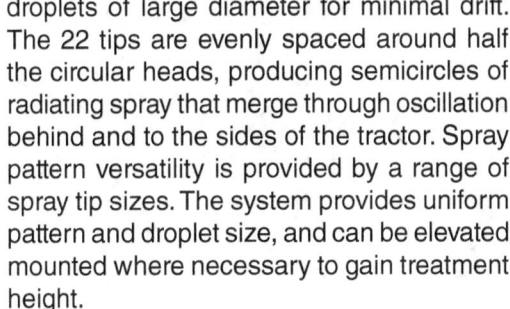

Radiarc® Sprayer 22-tip head.

Radiarc® Sprayer produces uniform large droplets.

Tractor-Mounted Wetblade and Cut-Spray Mower Applicators

Wetblade and cut-spray mowers are similar to "bush hogs" except herbicide is applied during or immediately after the cutting operation. One tractor-powered system dispenses herbicide onto the lower blade surface that wipes it onto the stems at the time of cutting. Control is inconsistent with this technology. Another system features an after-compartment behind the cutting deck that sprays herbicide onto the cut stems. The task of mowing and applying herbicides takes place in two specialized chambers. In the first chamber (the mower deck), the brush encounters a set of 6-inch blades capable of cutting stems 2 to 3 inches in diameter. The mowed debris is removed from the mowing chamber through a side discharge, not allowing the cut biomass to pass through the herbicide application chamber. Behind the mowing chamber is an enclosed herbicide chamber where the cut stubble encounters two treatment phases—a row of nozzles spray herbicide directly onto and through the stubble, not on the ground. Any herbicide that passes by the stubble is caught by an applicator consisting of scrapers, brushes, and chains; the applicator wipes herbicide onto the stubble in the second application stage. These systems assure precise herbicide application to the mowed area and prevent spray drift.

Wetblade mower systems also can deliver some biocontrol agents. Under certain conditions, this capability can integrate biological with mechanical control of invasives. Wetblade devices also can be added to normal brush saws for simultaneous cutting and treating of stumps.

Backpack Mist Blowers

Broadcast applications can be made with a gasoline-powered backpack mist blower. A wind turbine creates fine droplets that penetrate into shrubby stands and onto the foliage, but these droplets readily drift with wind and fog. As a safeguard to nontarget plants, foliar-active herbicides are usually recommended. These applications are only suitable for internal lands with dense infestations where drift of the mist-spray drops will be intercepted by target foliage and not move to nontarget plants or lands. Wind is critical for controlling this application. Wind must be minimal and moving away from a lane or spot of application into the target foliage. Applications must cease when gusts begin to occur. Privets have been treated successfully with this method in winter using a glyphosate herbicide when the hardwood overstory was mainly without leaves.

Wetblade brush mower applies herbicide while cutting.

Steven T. Manning

Wetblade system with two cutting heads.

Steven T. Manning

Backpack mist blower.

Tractor-Mounted Weed Wick

Applicators consist of a wick or rope soaked with herbicide from a reservoir fed by a manual-use handle or electrical pump. The wetted wick wipes herbicide over the leaves and stems of herbaceous invasive plants as it passes over them. Rope-wick and canvas-wick applicators have been used for decades in crop management, especially to control Johnsongrass [*Sorghum halepense* (L.) Pers.] with glyphosate herbicides. Longitudinal rope-wick applicators are robust and provide a long contact time between wicks and individual plants. Both the backs and sides of plants are treated. Canvas-wick and transverse rope-wick applicators are less expensive but are easily damaged in rough terrain and only apply herbicide to the back side of the plants with short contact time.

Roadside Sprayers

Roadside sprayers are an array of specially designed and constructed sprayers for treating linear roadsides at relatively high speeds and with minimal wind drift. These spray systems are mounted on trucks and have 500- to 3,000-gallon spray and mixing tanks. Herbicide metering systems regulate herbicide dispersal rates in synch with truck speed. Integrated boomless nozzle systems consist of multiple nozzle arrays for treating different sections of road rights-of-way. Where this method is approved by State departments of transportation or county commissioners, roadside sprayers are effective against invasive plants on the outer edge of rights-of-way.

Aerial Sprayers

Helicopter sprayers can apply herbicides on large or remote sites of extensive plant infestations. The helicopter blades can be folded for transport while mobile tanks with landing pads on top can permit operations from woods roads and openings. Helicopter applications to kudzu [*Pueraria montana* (Lour.) Merr.] infestations have been common and successful. More recently, dormant season helicopter applications of glyphosate have controlled Chinese privet growing in the shrub layer of hardwood forests absent of leaves. With GPS technology, helicopter applicators are extremely precise in treating target areas with preprogram swaths. They are highly maneuverable and apply sprays at much slower speeds than fixed-wing aircraft. Spray tanks vary in size from 90 to 230 gallons. Many types and sizes of nozzles are used, including control droplet and invert emulsion systems that minimize or eliminate spray drift. Contract aerial applicators are available in every part of the southern region.

Three types of tractor-mounted wick applicators

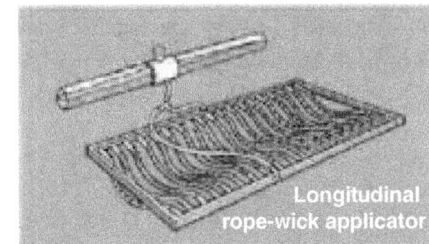
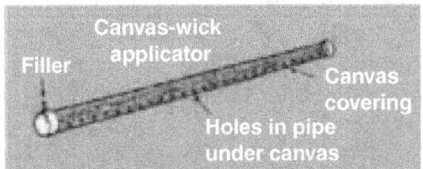
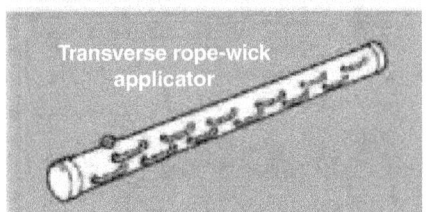

©Western Australian Agriculture Authority 2008

Roadside sprayers can treat invasives along highways.

Aerial spraying kudzu.

John D. Byrd

Fixed-wing aircraft sprayers have spray booms mounted below the lower wing. With payload capabilities and airspeeds both greater than that of helicopters, fixed-wing aircraft sprayers have been effective in controlling brush and weeds in large areas since the 1950s. Spray tank capacities vary from 400 to 800 gallons. GPS/GIS systems are used for precision applications. Fixed-wing planes are not suited for spraying highly irregular-shaped sites or mountainous areas and require a nearby airport. Many herbicides are not labeled for application by fixed-wing aircraft.

Large fixed-wing aircraft applicators include specially modified C–130H aircraft and Modular Aerial Spray Systems (MASS). MASS are designed for specially modified C–130 aircraft that spray biting insects such as mosquitoes, sand fleas, and filth flies. The systems also control vegetation growth on military bombing ranges. Although such services are available nationwide, there are few management areas sizeable enough to utilize such a service in the Eastern United States. As an example, one project conducted by the 910th Airlift Wing, U.S. Air Force Reserve, in Youngstown, OH, sprayed 2,880,662 acres, or 4,501 square miles—an area equivalent to the State of Connecticut. Fourteen thousand gallons of pesticides were used, and the missions comprised 191.4 hours of total flying time with 46.5 hours of actual "spray-on" time flying at 150 feet aboveground level. Future use on military reservations and extensive invasive plant infested lands is possible, since the system has been perfected.

C-130H aircraft and Modular Aerial Spray Systems (MASS).

Manual Methods

Manual methods include hand pulling as well as use of a wide array of tools for cutting, chopping, wrenching, and girdling invasive plants. Manual methods are mostly used on woody invasive plants when they are small. Eradication is only possible when the root crown or roots that can sprout are completely extracted and seedlings are pulled or eliminated following seed germination. Because it is difficult and even impossible to extract all of the shallow roots, stolons, and rhizomes of many invasives, resprouting will usually occur. Merely pulling small plants and cutting top growth will result only in short-term control before stump or root sprouting occurs, unless a herbicide is applied to cut surfaces.

When using manual methods, wear gloves, a long-sleeved shirt, long pants, and eye protection. Several invasive plants can cause skin irritation, especially among sensitive individuals. Some invasive species have thorns and sharp branches that are eye hazards, as well as flying soil from wrenching and digging that might enter the eye and warrant wearing safety glasses.

Hand pulling can be readily performed on seedlings of invasive woody plants (and some large herbaceous invasives) when soils are moist or loose. If the roots are completely extracted, then eradication is possible. But hand pulling will disturb the soil, creating a seedbed for other surrounding invasive plants that might be establishing in the site. This problem can be reduced by firming the soil with your boots and replanting dislodged desirable plants.

Hand pulling privet.

Hand clippers are useful for cutting back climbing vines and small multi-stemmed woody plants up to 1 inch in diameter. Cut as closely to the ground as possible. For vines, remove a 4- to 5-foot section to prevent regrowth trellising to the upper dead vine. Immediately apply an appropriate herbicide to the surface of the cut stem. When this is not an option, you will need to cut when resprouts appear, and do so repeatedly until no more regrowth. For most invasive vines with large roots, it is nearly impossible to deplete root energy reserves with repeated cutting. The most effective time for cutting is late spring when root reserves are lowest following spring emergence and growth. Clippers also can help gain access in dense brush where it is necessary to use other methods like backpack sprays. Purchase good quality clippers that have a bright color for easy locating and a holster for quick access. Always keep cutting tools sharpened, and carry sharpening stones and files to the field. Clean and maintain tools to prevent rust and provide safe operations.

Loppers are long-handled shears for cutting woody stems up to several inches in diameter. Sturdy long handles, handgrips, and ratchet mechanisms can increase the stem-size cutting capability. Cuts should be positioned as close to the ground as possible to effectively remove most stem buds. Loppers are commonly used in combination with a herbicide spray bottle for treating the cut-stump to prevent resprouting.

Loppers for vine cutting.

Three-tined pronghoe, pick mattocks, and folding hand pruning saws are used in combination by the Spartanburg Kudzu Coalition (www.kokudzu.com) to surgically remove kudzu root crowns. The knot or ball structure near the soil surface contains buds for both vine and root growth. When the root crown is extracted with these or other tools, the plant is killed. There is no need to dig up the long tuberous roots of kudzu as they contain no vine buds for regrowth.

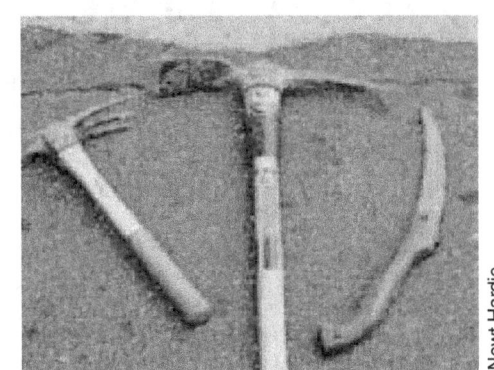

Machetes, bush axes, and cane knives are useful tools for both gaining access in thick brush as well as cutting plants for herbicide stem injection and cut-treat. Solid, easy-to-grip handles, hand guards, and easy-to-sharpen blades are best.

Manual tools for kudzu root crown extraction.

Shrub wrenches use a lever attached to a stem gripping device and a foot for extraction of woody root crowns. Shrub wrenches rely on operator weight or strength to uproot nonnative plants. These extraction tools are best suited for plants with shallow root systems, such as bush honeysuckle, Chinese privet, and other plants less than 3 inches in groundline diameter. Some brand names include the Weed Wrench™, Honeysuckle Popper, Root Talon, and Extractigator™. Shrub wrenches vary by weight, the pulling power, the size of plant that they can handle, and their foot size. Weight is a prime consideration for packing into remote locations. Pulling power of shrub wrenches currently available on the market range from 6:1 to 24:1. As an illustration of this ratio, an operator who applies 10 pounds of leverage force to the lever handle of a shrub wrench with a 12:1 pulling power ratio exerts 120 pounds of uprooting force to the plant. Foot size determines the kinds of soils the shrub wrench can be used in. Root extraction with a shrub wrench is easiest in soft soil, but working in soft soil also might hinder leverage with certain models because of the foot size and sinking into the soil. Soil disturbance and subsequent erosion can occur on steep slopes when wrenches are used.

A shrub wrench enhances human strength by the lever.

Select the right size shrub wrench to match the shrub size.

34

Girdling tools can control some invasive tree and shrub species, although this treatment is marginally effective. Both mechanical and gas-powered girdling tools are available specifically for girdling trees. Other girdling tools include chainsaws, axes, and levered chains. Girdling should penetrate the outer bark to completely sever the inner bark in a ring extending entirely around the trunk. An inch-wide strip of inner bark should be removed to stop flow of sap and nutrients in the stem. Most often a herbicide must be added to the cut area to stop stem and root resprouting. Girdling may result in additional hazards as subsequent dead standing trees decay and fall over time; therefore, girdling is not recommended in high-use areas (along trails or around structures).

Steven T. Manning

Ringer tree girdler.

Mechanical Methods

In many situations, hand labor is unavailable or cost prohibitive and more horsepower is needed. Developed for forestry and land clearing operations, mechanical methods use machines to clear large or dense infestations. Skid-steer loaders, mulchers, and tractors and bulldozers having special attachments have been used to reduce invasive woody plants. These methods can complement and increase the efficiency of herbicide treatments. Mechanical methods include root-raking attachments on bulldozers for preparing land for construction, landscaping, and other development. Heavy machinery root raking has eliminated privet thickets and kudzu patches (the uprooted plants are subsequently piled up and burned). Land clearing methods have also been used in large restoration projects when infestations are extensive and dense, followed by herbicide applications to resprouts and seedlings followed by revegetation with desirable plants. Some equipment, with appropriate attachments, can prepare the site for seeding and tree planting. Most important is using the appropriate size equipment to meet job requirements and minimize damage to soils and streams. Equipment and attachments include:

- Skid-steer loaders (modified for kudzu removal)
- Four-wheel drive tractors with brush mower, mulcher, harrow, seeder, seed drill, and tree planting attachments
- Mulchers (masticators)
- Bulldozers with sheer blade, root rake, ripper, harrow, combination plow, tree planter, fire plow, and grubber attachments

Timely followup with other control methods is essential, because disturbance of the soil creates favorable conditions for regrowth from seeds and root fragments. Mechanical removal with larger equipment may not be appropriate in natural areas unless the situation for restoration is critical because of special habitat and restoration plan requirements.

Skid-Steer Loaders

Paul David Blakely of the Coalition to Control Kudzu without Chemicals, a nonprofit volunteer organization in Spartanburg, SC, has developed attachments and techniques that equip skid-steer loaders for kudzu removal (http://kokudzu.com/SkidSteer-Loader.html). Tracks attached to the tires of the loader help traction and access to difficult terrain. Additional and wider spaced pronged forks added to the skid loader are inserted beneath the mat of vines, lifted up, and tilted back to pull vines and even kudzu root crowns for removal. Forward motion of the machine can roll the mass of vines into a pile. Other attachments and techniques have been developed by Blakely and the coalition for a range of conditions and treatment objectives. Skid loaders are easily transported, highly maneuverable, and capable of lift and tilt, which gives this machine, if equipped with appropriate attachments, potential for other invasive plant removal tasks in dense infestations.

Four-Wheel Drive Tractors

For decades, right-of-way and forestry managers have used specially equipped four-wheel drive tractors to apply an array of vegetation management treatments. The advantages of a tractor (over heavier machinery) include good traction for pulling implements in steep terrain and moderately wet soils, versatility of power takeoff (rear power shaft) to drive implements, convenient transportability, and low operation costs. A tractor must have a substantial cab guard to prevent penetration of stray tree limbs into the operator's cab area and keep the operator safe in the event of rollover and other accidents.

Depending on its size and configuration, a tractor can have a wide range of implements. A tractor can pull mowers and push mulcher attachments that reduce the height of herbaceous and woody invasive plants, prevent seed production, open up access for herbicide applicators, and otherwise prepare sites for further treatment. Tractors can pull plows and harrows that prepare soil, and seeders, seed drills, and fertilizer spreaders that can establish and promote growth of desirable plants. It can pull planting machinery for reforestation to plant pine and hardwood seedlings, and possibly native grass plugs. Tractors are often used to mount or pull herbicide sprayers. With this versatility the four-wheel-drive tractor is gaining favor as one of the most valuable pieces of machinery for integrated treatments aimed at restoration.

Skidloader with tracks and wider spaced pronged forks.

Skidloader uprooting kudzu vines for removal.

Invasive shrub being pulled by a small tractor.

Four-wheel-drive tractor with a boomless sprayer.

Mulchers and Mulching Attachments

Mulchers and mulching tractor attachments are increasingly preferred for reducing both standing invasive and native woody plants in dense infestations. Mulching machines are best for nonselective situations where the cost of selective control is prohibitive. Mulching machines are land clearing tools that can cut through dense stands of nonnative plants, reducing them to small pieces of woody debris. A one-operator machine can frequently cover 2 to 4 acres a day depending upon the terrain, vegetation type, and job requirements. Mulchers are designed as a single machine, while mulching attachments can be mounted on many types of equipment, tracked or wheeled, and even on the end of an articulated swing boom. The boom mount results in less trafficking damage to the soil because front-mounted mulchers must travel back and forth across the treatment area. The two basic types of mulching designs are vertical shaft and horizontal shaft. Either type can be equipped with pivoting flail-type cutters or rigidly mounted cutting teeth. Cutter types vary in the size of their shredded output, with smaller and faster rotating teeth producing the smallest size.

Mulchers can clear understory shrubs.

Steven T. Manning

Tracked mulching machine.

Dana Mitchell

Boom-mounted mulcher head.

John Klepac

Mulching machine with vertical shaft and pivoting flail-type cutters.

John Klepac

Mulching machine with horizontal shaft and rigid cutting teeth.

Dana Mitchell

After a mulched area has dried and regrowth occurs, prescribed burning can be used to reduce the surface mass, while herbicides can be more efficiently applied to the resprouts. Klepac and others (2007) reported on a trial of mulching dense Chinese privet followed by Garlon 3A herbicide applications to the stumps. Subsequent applications of foliar sprays to resprouts were required because stumps were often hidden by debris, with a total cost of $737 per acre. Mulching is currently a fairly expensive operation, but costs should decrease as the number of competing contractors increases.

Bulldozers

Bulldozers (or tracked tractors) are made in a range of sizes, and the larger ones have played roles in forestry operations for decades. Highly developed bulldozer attachments equip them for residual tree sheering and piling after timber harvest, soil preparation, tree planting, and fire line plowing. These same operations have found use in large-scale invasive plant reclamation projects tackling extensive woody infestation, although smaller tractors and implements are used. The amount of soil disturbance and compaction is considerable with bulldozers, varying by equipment size, soil moisture, number of passes, stand density, and tree/shrub size, but often less than with wheeled tractors. The ground pressure of tracks is less than with wheeled equipment.

Gena Todia

Bulldozer scrapes and piles Chinese privet.

Attachments for bulldozers are described below:

- Sheer blades are usually mounted at an angle to forward travel with a lower jutting serrated dozer blade that fells trees when pushed against them.

- Brush rakes and root rakes are blades with extending lower teeth that dislodge surface roots and stumps of smaller trees. Brush rakes have been used in restoration to clear dense large privet stands in preparation for other treatments before native tree and grass planting.

- Rippers are thick steel shanks mounted on the sides of bulldozers to penetrate and loosen the soil and subsoil with forward motion along an intended tree planting row. This treatment is done before tree planting to facilitate root penetration and growth where there are plowpans or hardpans in the soil. However, the benefits for pine establishment in the South have been reported to be minimal, except on particularly rocky soils.

- Disk harrows are gangs of disks often pulled in tandem across a harvested or cleared site to loosen surface soils and incorporate organic debris for more rapid decomposition and to facilitate planting.

- Combination plows are pulled behind the tractor and can have a ripping shank, colter, wing plow, and/or offset disk harrows on the same implement depending upon the soil conditions. Soils are both loosened and piled within an intended tree or shrub planting row to benefit early survival and growth.

- Bedding plows are most useful in seasonally wet coastal sites for raising tree planting rows to prevent water logging and to concentrate scarce soil nutrients.

- Tree planters are pulled behind a tracked or wheeled tractor with implements that form a planting slit and then close it after the operator riding in the planter inserts a tree seedling or seedling plug. Native plant seedlings can potentially be planted with this machine for restoration.

- Fire plows are pulled behind a tracked or wheeled tractor that clears and parts surface soils in a wide path (several feet across) to a depth of about 6 inches. This fire line of bare soil can be used to set a backfire in preparation for prescribed burning or stopping wildfires.

- Grubbers are sharp, U-shaped blades mounted on the front of crawler tractors, wheel loaders, excavators, or farm tractors to uproot individual trees or large shrubs. Other units clamp onto the tree and pull the tree from the soil. The size and type of tractor depends on the size of trees to be grubbed and the terrain. Units are commercially available, but many are fabricated in welding shops. Farm tractors with small, three-point hitch grubbers are popular for use on limited acreages of previously cleared areas. Grubbing is not practical in rocky soil or when tree densities are greater than 250 per acre over extensive acreages. With care, selectivity is afforded with this method, while soil disturbance is great.

Sheer blade on a bulldozer.

Brush rake attachment for a bulldozer.

Rootrake on a bulldozer.

Ripper shank on bulldozer in the up position.

Wildland off-set disks.

Combination plow with a ripper shank in the center, a wing plow behind, and four disk harrows.

Bedding plow with compacting roller used to raise the soil in a planting row.

Tree planter attachment.

If not planned and enacted with care, mechanical root raking and disking can intensify and spread infestations of invasive plants that have runners by chopping the runners into resprouting segments. All mechanical equipment used in treating invasive plant infestation can transport seeds, roots, rhizomes, and spores to other sites. Equipment inspection and cleaning is essential to stop subsequent invasive plant spread.

Cultural Methods

Several cultural practices, including prescribed burning and water-level manipulation, can reduce or control nonnative invasive plant populations. However, such practices also may have undesirable impacts to soils, animal habitat, and native species, so care in planning and enactment must be exercised.

Prescribed Burning

Fire has played a critical and natural role in the development and maintenance of grasslands, forests, and wetlands throughout history. Prescribed burning is the deliberate use of fire under specified and controlled conditions to achieve a resource management goal. Most States train burn specialists through a certified prescribed burn managers program and require that those who contract burning have certification for providing liability protection. Like other invasive treatments, prescribed burning requires special skills and experience, including smoke management, for effective and safe implementation. A prescribed burning plan must include clearly stated objectives, the ignition approach, equipment and manpower needs, and mitigation measures. Additionally, a permit is required from State or local agencies before burning. Prescribed burning for invasive plant management has advantages and disadvantages.

Advantages of prescribed burning for invasive plant control—

Privet, fire girdled.

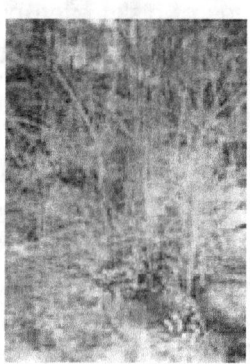
Privet respouts after burn.

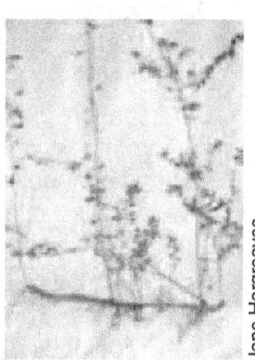
Chinese privet sprouts along root.

Jane Hargreaves

1. Per acre, prescribed burning is one of the most inexpensive treatments.
2. Top growth of herbaceous invasive plants can be consumed and small woody plants can be fire girdled, resulting in resprouts of lower heights. Resprouts of trees, shrubs, and vines then can be more easily treated with herbicide foliar sprays.
3. Some seeds of invasive plants can be consumed in the burn.
4. Prescribed burns improve access to the treatment site and expose hazards, such as stumps, sinkholes, old wells, and pits that might otherwise hinder or endanger further operations.
5. Prescribed burns can clear thatch and shrubs for more effective herbicide applications.

Disadvantages of prescribed burning for invasive plant control—

1. Prescribed burning requires special skills and experience, investments in time for training and certification, and purchase of special equipment.
2. Results are variable and can be unexpected when fire escapes.
3. Abundant resprouts and seedlings of invasives along with native regrowth can exacerbate conditions for subsequent treatments and jeopardize their success.
4. Prescribed burns can stimulate flowering and seeding of some invasive plants, such as cogongrass, and scarify seeds of others, such as lespedezas (*Lespedeza* spp.), to promote enhanced germination.
5. Some invasive plants can burn extremely hot and intense, with vines creating ladder fuels, placing fire crews in jeopardy, killing or injuring desirable plants, and increasing chances of fire escape.

Cogongrass rhizomes have been spread by fireplows.

Japanese climbing fern burns into tree and shrub tops by fuel ladders.

Chuck Bargeron

6. Litter clearing and loss of stand components like shrubs can make the site more prone for reinvasion or invasion by other species.
7. Plowing fire lines can spread invasive plants and make soil susceptible to invasion and soil erosion.

Prescribed burn effectiveness—

The effectiveness of a prescribed burn depends on the intensity and timing relative to target plant size and development. Fire intensity is determined by the amount of fuel and its arrangement and dryness, along with weather, topography, and ignition source and pattern. Prescribed burns are usually ignited by drip torches, initially along plowed or disked fire lines to widen the fire break. Then the area is ignited as a ring-fire technique around the perimeter or as strip (or spot) headfires or backfires working with or against the wind direction.

The most effective time for weakening woody invasive plants is burning in the late spring after plants have initiated growth using root reserves. Burning in late winter or spring leaf-out can minimize the period of bare soil, while summer burns are the hottest and can maximize consumption of standing plants. Burning can predispose a forest stand or opening to invasion, even though prescribed burning increasingly is favored for native plant and longleaf pine ecosystem restoration as well as fuel reduction. A close evaluation of the benefits and risks is demanded before applying prescribed burning.

Fire lines contain prescribed burns and are the base for backfires.

Igniting a strip-headfire with a drip torch.

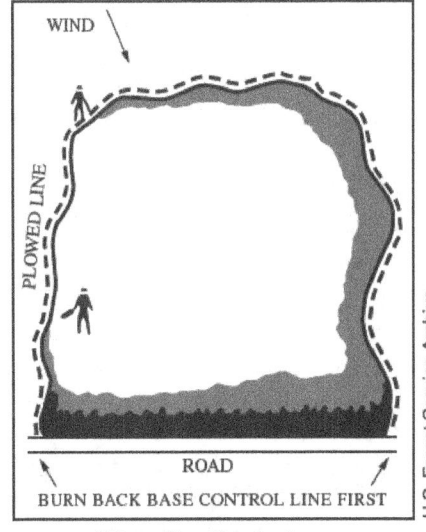

Ring Fire Technique

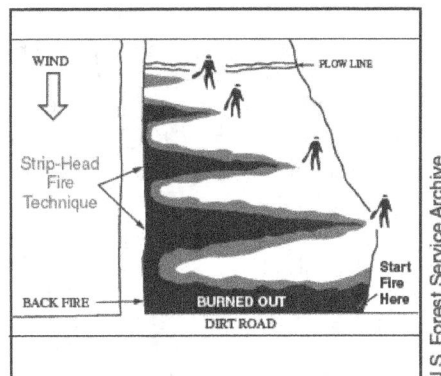

Flamers or Spot Burners

Fire from a propane spot burner can be used to kill individual or small groups of invasive plants. Commercial kits are available for attaching propane cylinders to a backpack frame and fitting the cylinder with a flame nozzle. Additionally, tractor mounted units have also been developed. When plant and wet fuel conditions permit, the flame is directed at herbaceous and woody invasives. This operation can be convenient since it can be performed in wet conditions and when fuels are low. Best results are obtained under windless conditions as winds can prevent the heat from reaching the target weeds. For further details, refer to the The Nature Conservancy's "Weed Control Methods Handbook" appendix at http://www.invasive.org/gist/products/handbook/23.Spotburn.pdf.

Propane spot burners treating garlic mustard.

Water-Level Manipulation

In areas where water level can be manipulated, flooding or drawdowns can reduce invasive plant species in aquatic and wetland habitats but is usually not effective as a stand-alone treatment. This method is species and site specific. For effective outcomes, managers must first understand the biology of both invasive and native plants in the treatment area. Water-level manipulation works by either lowering water levels to kill invasive plants that cannot tolerate exposure to dry and hot conditions or raising water levels to kill invasive plants that cannot tolerate submergence or water-logged soils. However, both processes can spread floating seeds of invasives and make habitats more vulnerable to nonnative plant establishment. Lowered water levels in spring and summer can also facilitate herbicide applications in wetlands for controlling such plants as alligatorweed [*Alternanthera philoxeroides* (Mart.) Griseb.].

Alligatorweed herbicide sprayed after lake level lowered.

Biological Control Methods

Biological control, or biocontrol, of plants uses living organisms to weaken, kill, or stop seed production of a targeted invasive plant. The most common agents in biocontrol programs are insects and pathogens, and uses of nematodes and mites are under study.

Classical biocontrol involves finding agents in the home range or similar habitat of the invasive plant, followed by intensive research on feeding habits and reproduction, and a planned introduction of plant-specific agents into invaded areas. The goal is to identify predators that are host specific to the target invasives, i.e., they will not attack native plants, and will increase and spread in the new range to permanently suppress the invasive species. Classical biocontrol has an initially high public cost due to an often lengthy search for the right agent, extensive feeding tests in special quarantine facilities, coordinated releases, and long-term monitoring. There are specific requirements through a series of scheduled oversights by a Federal Government interagency committee requiring documented studies to strictly control biocontrol agent releases. Following release, nontarget damage is very rare but has occurred with the classic example of the musk thistle head weevil (*Rhinocyllus conicus* Frölich, 1792) attacking native thistles. In general, scientific evaluations of past releases have shown that the benefits from biocontrol over a region outweigh the detriments.

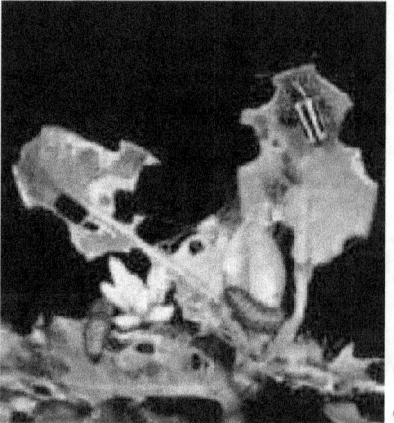

Gary Buckingham

Agasicles hygrophila adults and larvae devour leaves and upper portions of stems

Classical biocontrol programs in the southern region are under development for tallowtree [*Triadica sebifera* (L.) Roxb.], Chinese privet, and tropical soda apple (*Solanum viarum* Dunal), and in Florida for Old World climbing fern also known as small-leaf climbing fern [*Lygodium microphyllum* (Cav.) R. Br.]. Successful projects underway target purple loosestrife (*Lythrum salicaria* L.), melaleuca [*Melaleuca quinquenervia* (Cav.) S.F. Blake], and alligatorweed.

Augmentative and inundative biocontrol identifies native insects, pathogens, nematodes, and mites that feed upon nonnative invasive plants in this country. When the appropriate agents are discovered and researched, there is an attempt to release large numbers of them into high infestation areas of the invasive plant. A program under development for kudzu uses this method. This program and other prior efforts have used pathogens and have been formulated into sprays, often referred to as bioherbicides. The challenge has been to maintain the viability of the pathogen or spores during packaging, shipment, application, and residence on the target foliage.

Prescribed Grazing

Prescribed grazing is an approach that relies on cattle, sheep, goats, and horses to reduce infestations. Grazing is a potential control treatment when the invasive is palatable and the invasive plant is not poisonous to the animal. Cattle and horses are useful for many herbaceous invasive plants, while sheep and goats will feed on woody plants as well. Goats will defoliate and debark shrubs, saplings, and small trees to a higher level than sheep, even thorny vegetation. The animal species is important as is the breed, the best being those breeds that are larger and can handle difficult grazing and browsing conditions.

Horses grazing cogongrass.

Care of the herd is critical, and must include regular inspections, treatment of injuries, vaccinations, and water supply. Both shock grazing and year-round grazing have been researched and used to limited degrees. Multiple years are required to

achieve major invasive plant reductions and additional methods are required for restoration. Spring and early summer are critical times for goat and sheep control of invasive shrubs. The key to control is repeated heavy defoliation in spring and early summer without overgrazing grasses and legumes. Thus a rotation system works best. Using a mixture of goats, sheep, and cattle will provide the most effective clearing and subsequent plant kill, especially of multiflora rose (*Rosa multiflora* Thunb. ex Murr.) and autumn olive (*Elaeagnus umbellata* Thunb.). Goats are most useful for these woody species at 5 to 10 animals per acre during the first season, while fewer goats can be used after two or three seasons. All of these grazers and browsers have been used in kudzu control programs to varying degrees of success.

Hair sheep shock grazing kudzu after 2 days.

Goats browse young growth first.

Mulching and Solarization

Mulching for weed control is the use of materials to cover the soil surface that block light, thereby preventing weed germination and growth. While mulches and landscape fabrics are commonly used in restoration operations for reseeding and soil stabilization, mulches for weed control must be applied at rates high enough to prevent light from reaching the soil surface. Mulching is most effective on controlling small seeded species and is marginally effective on established resprouting perennials. There are many types of mulches including natural ones such as straw, bark, sawdust, crop residues, and grass clippings, and artificial ones such as paper, cardboard, and plastic. While mulch applications are not commonly made to control invasives on a large scale, they are still useful. For example, the use of a mulching machine for clearing privet and tallowtree can create a heavy mulch layer that will suppress subsequent seedling

Prescribed grazing by cattle for kudzu control before planting pines.

recruitment. Another effective use of mulch, especially to suppress dense ground covers, combines cardboard and organic mulch. The cardboard covers and over-laps edges of the treatment area, and is then covered with organic mulch. Small drain holes in the cardboard prevent water from pooling. Left to compost in place, the cardboard will suppress vegetation underneath.

Soil solarization uses polyethylene sheeting to cover low growing, cultivated, mowed, or chopped invasive infestations and trap solar energy to heat the soil and space under the sheeting to kill and suppress invasive plants. At least 2 years of summer cover are needed to suppress most invasives plants by 90 percent. Other plants are killed by this method—it is not selective. Black sheeting is more effective than clear sheeting because it blocks needed sunlight, and, at an extra cost, is available with UV blockers to greatly extend the useful life of sheets to more than one growing season. Sheeting costs range from $1,500 to $3,500 per acre, while the labor costs of installation have not been reported. Sheets can be held in place with soil mounds and squares of old carpet. A detriment is the mosquitoes that breed in rainwater puddles that form on sheets. The method is useful as a first treatment for relatively small areas and where herbicides cannot be used. Summer is the most effective season, and use on wet soils increases control. After removal, the bare soil is open for reinvasion unless desirable re-vegetation is gained.

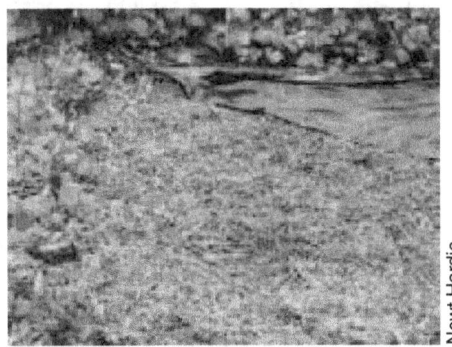

Black polyethylene sheet first removed from kudzu.

One month later, surviving kudzu sprouts.

Rehabilitation, Restoration, and Reclamation

The promotion and establishment of desirable vegetation during the latter phases of control and eradication treatments is one of the most important phases of an integrated invasive plant management program. The severity of infestation, site degradation, and desired future outcome determine whether a rehabilitation, restoration, or more stringent reclamation effort is required.

Rehabilitation is used when soil, stream, and wetland damage is minimal and native plants are present or will enter from surrounding areas for reestablishment. Native tree species that grow fast, e.g., genetically improved loblolly pine seedlings, can be planted to suppress invasive plant regrowth. Restoration is a much more involved process of using soil and streambank stabilization methods with planting and seeding of desirable species to create a planned stable landscape. Reclamation is used on surface-mined lands, large road construction projects, and other severely altered sites to reshape landform, replace surface soils, and plant or seed rapidly growing plants often using mulches and fertilizers. Invasive plants have been most often planted on reclamation sites and now warrant control efforts. Native or noninvasive plants are recommended substitutes now available for reclamation operations.

Loblolly pine plantation in sixth growing season established in a 10-year-old cogongrass infestation after a herbicide suppression treatment.

The goal of all three approaches is the establishment and/or release of fast-growing native plants that can outcompete and outlast any surviving nonnative plants while stabilizing and protecting the soil and water features. At times, nonnative plants must be used to suppress invasives, then controlled, to facilitate native plant establishment.

Containerized native plants for restoration plantings.

If the soil seed bank remains intact, native plant communities will naturally re-initiate succession during eradication of nonnative plants. Light-seeded native species are usually present in the seed bank while heavier seeded plants will gradually be deposited on a site by birds and other animals. Select herbicides and other treatments such as mowing and prescribed burning can play roles in continued suppression of invasives while promoting native or noninvasive plants.

Herbicide Use in Restoration of Native Grasses

Matt Nespeca, Executive Director of the Conservation Land Company in Charleston, SC, notes that, in the restoration of native grasses, herbicides can increase survival and growth of desirable native grasses and forbs, while reducing cover of invasive plants. It is important to know what plants a herbicide can control on a site, but it is even more important to understand what plants a herbicide will not control. On a restoration site, the idea of herbicide application selectivity (or the susceptibility or tolerance of a plant to a herbicide application) can be attained through herbicide spectrum, herbicide placement, or herbicide timing. Over the past several years, these methods have been used on native grass restoration projects throughout South Carolina, including Mepkin Abbey, McAlhaney Preserve, and Rock Hill Black Jack Heritage Preserve.

Seeding and mulching to establish desirable species.

Ben Jackson

In some native grass restoration projects, a manager can rely on herbicide spectrum to provide selectivity. When bahiagrass is outcompeting an established stand of native big bluestem (*Andropogon gerardii* Vitman) and little bluestem [*Schizachyrium scoparium* (Michx.) Nash], a manager can use a broadcast herbicide treatment of Escort XP Herbicide (metsulfuron) to reduce the bahiagrass competition and release the native grasses. If the same established stand of big bluestem and little bluestem is infested by Johnsongrass, Plateau Herbicide (imazapic) provides selective control of Johnsongrass but is safe for the native grasses. A more obvious method of utilizing a herbicide spectrum in native grass restoration is with broadleaf-specific products, such as Garlon 4 Ultra (triclopyr), which control broadleaf species while releasing grasses.

Herbicide placement, as it relates to native grass restoration, can be accomplished through directed foliar applications to undesirable plants while avoiding contact with desirable plants. For example, Roundup Pro (glyphosate) will control many grasses during the growing season, but a skilled applicator can still treat patches of Bermudagrass in a restoration area while avoiding contact with desirable nearby grasses.

Herbicide timing can be effective in controlling cool-season grasses with nonselective herbicides, such as Roundup Pro when warm-season grasses are in dormancy. Herbicide timing is also effective for midwinter applications when nonnative evergreen shrubs such as Chinese privet are invading highly diverse grassland habitats where safety for existing forbs and grasses is essential.

In recent years, native plant seed and seedlings have become increasingly available for sowing and planting, even though there is a limited number of species and well-developed establishment procedures. A number of individuals, agencies, and companies are collecting native seed to establish seed production areas. The Nature Conservancy is working in partnership with Roundstone Native Seed, LLC, to begin production and sale of cleaned seeds of local origin for restoration, reclamation, and wildlife habitats. A Web site by the Lady Bird Johnson Wildflower Center of the University of Texas at Austin includes a National Suppliers Directory of nearby native seed and plant sources: http://www.wildflower.org/suppliers/show.php?id=683.

Grass seed harvester on an ATV.

Special seed collection equipment is available for prairie mixtures and grasses. Seedling native plants can be also collected and transplanted from suitable field sites. Native plant seeds will require proper treatments to assure timely germination. Their establishment will be more challenging than the commonly available nonnative plants so often used for soil stabilization and wildlife food plots (see "Six Basic Elements for Successful Native Grass and Forb Establishment," by Randy Seymour, John Seymour, and Chris Blackford, Roundstone Native Seed, www.roundstoneseed.com). Listed in the appendix are "Nonnative Invasive Plant Species Not to be Used or Recommended for Wildlife Food Plots nor Bird and Butterfly Viewing Gardens" and "Low-Growing Native Plants with Potential for Southern Right-of-Way Stabilization and Beautification." Use of native plants for wildlife food plots and right-of-way stabilization is long overdue.

Grass seed harvester head.

Often fast-growing native tree and shrub species should be established during the latter control phase to hinder reestablishment of shade-intolerant nonnative invasive plants. Tree nurseries operated by State forestry agencies are a good source of many species of native trees and shrubs, while other commercial sources are scattered throughout the region.

Constant surveillance, maintaining forest vigor with minimal disturbance, treatment of new unwanted arrivals, and finally, promotion or establishment of plants during eradication is critical for managing invasions.

The Muddy Creek Restoration Project eradicates privets, tallowtree, and cogongrass with establishment of native plants.

Management Strategies and Herbicide Prescriptions for Invasive Plants

The following are management strategies and herbicide prescription summaries for prevalent invasive plants, detailing mainly selective application treatments. These management strategies and prescriptions have been assembled from published research results, unpublished trials, State reports, weed council manuals, magazines, and Web sites. In general, few species-specific experiments have been reported that compare a full array of treatments for invasive plant species. But until further specific understanding is gained, we must proceed with current knowledge and technology to manage their invasions. **Herbicides are mentioned in order by effectiveness when comparative information is available or alphabetically when such information is lacking.** Remember to not exceed the label-specified maximum herbicide amounts per acre, especially when using selective application treatments.

Invasive tree species hinder reforestation and management of rights-of-way and natural areas as well as dramatically alter habitats. Some species occur initially as scattered trees and eventually form dense stands if not controlled. Most spread by prolific seed production and abundant root sprouts. Depending on conditions, they can be eliminated with herbicides by stem injection, cut-treat, soil spots, basal sprays, and foliar sprays. Following stem control, total elimination requires surveillance and treatment of root sprouts and plant germinants that originate from the soil seed bank.

Brazilian Peppertree

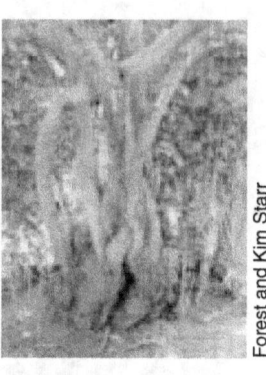

Michael Jordan

Steven T. Manning

Forest and Kim Starr

Brazilian peppertree (*Schinus terebinthifolius* Raddi) is an evergreen shrub or small tree to 40 feet (12 m) in height that often grows in dense infestations and has many short trunks or arching stems of contorted branches. Drooping, odd-pinnately compound leaves smell of turpentine when crushed. Many multibranched clusters of small whitish flowers appear in summer and fall that yield abundant clusters of spherical red pepper-smelling fruit in winter (only on female plants). Seed is produced as early as 3 years. Germination mainly occurs November to April, with seed viability ranging from 30 to 60 percent. Seedling mortality is mostly due to drought.

Seed is spread mainly by birds, but also by ground animals, gravity, and water. Seedlings can establish in shade, but open disturbed areas are most susceptible to invasion. Infestations intensify by many root sprouts that yield entangled stems and branches with abundant foliage having allelopathic chemicals. Burning is intense due to chemicals in the foliage, and can destroy seeds as well as result in basal and root sprouts that can outgrow native species. The species range is presently limited to Florida and extreme south Texas, but with warming trends, spread northward is projected.

Management strategies:
- Cut when seeds are not present and avoid contacting the inter-bark since a rash can result. Seeds appear only on female plants.
- Minimize disturbance in areas where this plant occurs.
- Treat when new plants are young to prevent seed formation.
- Manually pull new seedlings and tree wrench saplings when soil is moist, ensuring removal of all roots.
- Mechanical and burning treatments should be used with care and extra caution when done in conjunction with herbicide treatments.
- Treatment combinations should be used that are appropriate for dense thickets with limited access. Access trails may need to be cut.

Recommended control procedures:
Trees. For stems too tall for foliar sprays, cut large stems and immediately treat the stump tops with Garlon 3A or a glyphosate herbicide as a 25- to 50-percent solution (3 to 6 quarts per 3-gallon mix), Garlon 4 as a 12-percent solution (3 pints per 3-gallon mix), or Stalker* as a 12-percent solution (3 pints per 3-gallon mix) when not fruiting. ORTHO Brush-B-Gon and Enforcer Brush Killer are effective undiluted for treating cut-stumps and available in retail garden stores (safe to surrounding plants). For treatment of extensive infestations in forest situations, apply Velpar L* or Hyvar X-L* to the soil surface within 3 feet of the stem (one mL squirt per 1-inch stem diameter) or in a grid pattern at spacings and dilutions specified on the herbicide labels.
Saplings. Apply a basal spray of Garlon 4 as a 20-percent solution (5 pints per 3-gallon mix) in a labeled basal oil product, vegetable oil or mineral oil with a penetrant, or fuel oil or diesel fuel (where permitted); or apply undiluted Pathfinder II in the fall when saplings are flowering.
Seedlings and saplings. Thoroughly wet all leaves with one of the following herbicides in water with a surfactant: a glyphosate herbicide or Garlon 3A as a 2- to 3-percent solution (8 to 12 ounces per 3-gallon mix) or Arsenal AC* as a 0.5-percent solution (2 ounces per 3-gallon mix); and in wet pastures and aquatic sites, Habitat* as a 0.5- to 1-percent solution (2 to 4 ounces per 3-gallon mix) or Clearcast* as a 2-percent solution (8 ounces per 3-gallon mix).

---

* Nontarget plants may be killed or injured by root uptake.

Callery Pear, Bradford Pear

Callery pear or Bradford pear (*Pyrus calleryana* Decne.) is a widely planted deciduous tree to 60 feet (18 m) in height and with boles to 2 feet (0.6 m) in diameter. Major branches fork from trunk at narrow angles, and often split at the juncture after wind and ice storms. Leaves are ovate and long petioled, alternate, turn red in fall, and tufted on stubby thorned or nonthorned branchlets. Abundant small pears are typically present in fall and winter and are spread by birds and possibly other animals. Seed viability varies by location, and several commercial sterile varieties can cross-pollinate with certain other pear species in close proximity to produce fertile hybrids. Thickets and dense stands are formed by root sprouts. This species can tolerate partial shade and a variety of soils. Fruiting starts at 3 years.

Management strategies:
- Do not plant. Remove prior plantings, and control sprouts and seedlings. Bag and dispose of fruit in a dumpster or burn.
- Treat when new plants are young to prevent seed formation.
- Cut and bulldoze when fruit are not present.
- Manual pulling and tree wrenching is hindered by thorny branches and eye protection should be used.
- Manually pull new seedlings and tree wrench saplings when soil is moist, ensuring removal of all roots.
- Burning treatments are suspected of having minimal topkill effect due to scant litter.
- Treatment combinations should be used that are appropriate for dense thickets with limited access. Access trails may need to be cut.

Recommended control procedures:
Trees. For stems too tall for foliar sprays, cut large stems and immediately treat the stump tops with Garlon 3A or a glyphosate herbicide as a 25- to 50-percent solution (2 to 6 quarts per 3-gallon mix). ORTHO Brush-B-Gon and Enforcer Brush Killer are effective undiluted for treating cut-stumps and available in retail garden stores (safe to surrounding plants). Make stem injections using undiluted Garlon 3A during June through September in cut-spacings as specified on the herbicide label. A subsequent foliar application may be required to control new seedlings and resprouts.

Saplings. Apply Garlon 4 as a 20-percent solution (5 pints per 3-gallon mix) in a labeled basal oil product, vegetable oil or mineral oil with a penetrant, or fuel oil or diesel fuel (where permitted); or apply undiluted Pathfinder II to young bark as a basal spray. Basal spray applications can be made year-round.

Seedlings. Thoroughly wet all leaves with one of the following herbicides in water with a surfactant: a glyphosate herbicide or Garlon 3A as a 2-percent solution (8 ounces per 3-gallon mix), Arsenal AC* as a 0.25-percent solution (1 ounce per 3-gallon mix), or Arsenal PowerLine* as a 0.5-percent solution (2 ounces per 3-gallon mix).

---

* Nontarget plants may be killed or injured by root uptake.

Camphortree

  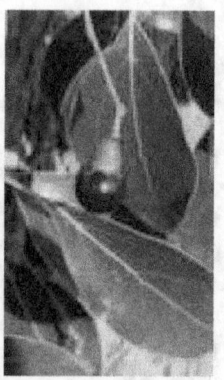  

Camphortree [*Cinnamomum camphora* (L.) J. Presl] is an evergreen tree 60 to 100 feet (18 to 30 m) in height, with boles up to 2 feet (0.6 m) in diameter and a round spreading crown formed by large branches radiating from midtree. Leaves are glossy, lanceolate, alternate at twig tips, and have a camphor odor when crushed, cut, or bruised. Twigs are slender, green-to-reddish brown. Abundant clusters of spherical, black drupes are present in fall to winter, and are spread by animals, water, and gravity. Colonizes by root sprouts and is found in dense thickets.

Management strategies:

- Do not plant. Remove prior plantings. Bag and dispose of fruit in a dumpster or burn.
- Treat when new plants are young to prevent seed formation.
- Cut and bulldoze when fruit are not present.
- Manually pull new seedlings and tree wrench saplings when soil is moist, ensuring removal of all roots.
- Burning treatments are useful for seedling and sapling topkill when leaflitter is present, and fires can be hot.

Recommended control procedures:

Large trees. Make stem injections using undiluted Garlon 3A (June through September) or Vanquish* as a 75-percent solution (9 quarts per 3-gallon mix) with water (June through November) in cut-spacings specified on the herbicide label. For stems too tall for foliar sprays, cut large stems and immediately treat the stump tops with Garlon 3A as a 30-percent solution (7 pints per 3-gallon mix) or Garlon 4 as a 25-percent solution (3 quarts per 3-gallon mix), and add a penetrant for more effective control. ORTHO Brush-B-Gon and Enforcer Brush Killer are effective undiluted for treating cut-stumps and available in retail garden stores (safe to surrounding plants).

Saplings. Apply a basal spray for trees up to 4 inches in diameter using Garlon 4 as a 30-percent solution (7 pints per 3-gallon mix) in a labeled basal oil product, vegetable oil or mineral oil with a penetrant, or fuel oil or diesel fuel (where permitted).

Seedlings and saplings. Thoroughly wet all leaves with one of the following herbicides in water with a surfactant: a glyphosate herbicide, Garlon 3A, Garlon 4, or Clearcast* for wetlands and aquatic sites, as 2-percent solutions (8 ounces per 3-gallon mix).

---

* Nontarget plants may be killed or injured by root uptake.

Chinaberrytree

 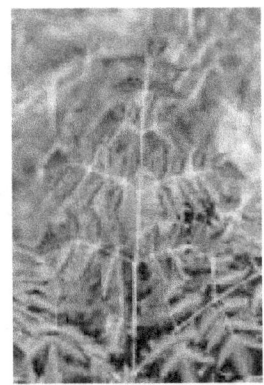  

Chinaberrytree (*Melia azedarach* L.) is a traditional widely escaped ornamental that is deciduous, growing to about 50 feet (15 m) tall. It has lacy, many divided leaves that are dark green, turning yellow in fall. Showy panicles of tiny blue flowers in spring yield abundant round yellow pulpy fruit that persist during winter. Stump sprouts, root sprouts, and seedlings will eventually emerge after main stems are killed. Viable seed can be produced by 4- and 5-year-old plants. Species spreads by abundant bird-dispersed seeds.

Management strategies:

- Remove old ornamental plantings, and control sprouts and seedlings. Bag and dispose of fruit in a dumpster or burn.
- Treat the abundant seedlings after parent tree is killed.
- Rapid growth requires foliar sprays in the first year.
- Cut and bulldoze when fruit are not present.
- Manually pull new seedlings and tree wrench saplings when soil is moist, ensuring removal of all roots.
- Burning treatments are suspected of having minimal topkill effect due to scant litter.

Recommended control procedures:

Trees. Using dilutions and cut-spacings specified on the herbicide label (anytime except March and April) make stem injections using Arsenal AC* or Pathway*, or when safety to surrounding vegetation is desired, Garlon 3A. For felled trees, apply these herbicides to stump tops immediately after cutting. Also, ORTHO Brush-B-Gon and Enforcer Brush Killer are effective undiluted for treating cut-stumps and available in retail garden stores (safe to surrounding plants).

Saplings. Apply a basal spray of Garlon 4 as a 10- to 20-percent solution (2 to 5 pints per 3-gallon mix) or Stalker* as a 3-percent solution (12 ounces per 3-gallon mix) plus Garlon 4 as a 15-percent solution (3.5 pints per 3-gallon mix) mixed in a labeled basal oil product, vegetable oil or mineral oil with a penetrant, or fuel oil or diesel fuel (where permitted).

Sprouts and seedlings. Thoroughly wet all leaves with one of the following herbicides in water with a surfactant (July to October): Garlon 3A or Garlon 4 as a 2-percent solution (8 ounces per 3-gallon mix) when safety to surrounding plants is desired; or Arsenal AC* as a 1-percent solution (4 ounces per 3-gallon mix), or Arsenal PowerLine* as a 0.5-percent solution (2 ounces per 3-gallon mix).

---

* Nontarget plants may be killed or injured by root uptake.

Chinese Parasoltree

  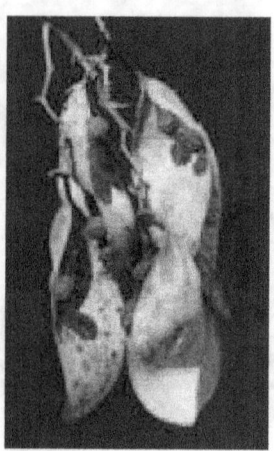 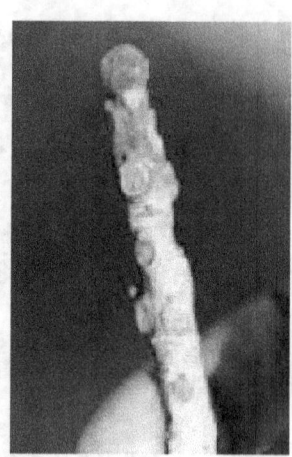

Chinese parasoltree [*Firmiana simplex* (L.) W. Wight] is an increasingly planted ornamental deciduous upright tree that grows up to 50 feet (16 m) in height. It has smooth, striped trunks to 2 feet (60 cm) in diameter with stout alternate branches. Leaves can be over 1 foot (30 cm) across, dark green above and fuzzy white beneath, and mostly three-to-five lobed with petioles almost as long as the leaf. Terminal large showy clusters of tan and yellow flowers appear in midsummer to quickly yield unusual pods that split into four leaflike sections (little boats) joined at the apex with several pea-sized fruit attached along the upper margins. Round oily seeds can germinate immediately after fully formed in winter in semitropical parts of Florida and the Gulf Coastal Plain or in the spring further north. Leaves turn yellow in fall, and multibranched showy fruit stalks remain over winter into early summer. An extremely rapid growing species with variegated cultivars advertised and sold for "instant shade." Abundant seeds per tree are highly viable and spread by wind and water to form surrounding infestations. Seedlings will persist in shade, growing rapidly tall to reach sunlight, while saplings and trees require partial to full sunlight. Many surface roots can lift sidewalks in urban plantings and sprout after tree kill. Capable of spread throughout the region.

Management strategies:

- Do not plant. Advise nurseries not to sell. Remove prior plantings. Bag and dispose of fruit in a dumpster or burn, and control seedlings.
- Treat when new plants are young to prevent seed formation.
- Cut and bulldoze when fruit are not present in spring and early summer.
- Manually pull new seedlings and tree wrench saplings when soil is moist, ensuring removal of all roots.
- Burning treatments are useful for seedling and sapling topkill when leaflitter is present and fires can be hot.

Recommended control procedures:

Large trees. Make stem injections using a glyphosate herbicide or Garlon 3A in dilutions and cut-spacings specified on the herbicide label. For stems too tall for foliar sprays, cut large stems and immediately treat the stump tops with a glyphosate herbicide or Garlon 3A as a 30-percent solution (7 pints per 3-gallon mix) or Garlon 4 as a 25-percent solution (3 quarts per 3-gallon mix), and add a penetrant for more effective control. ORTHO Brush-B-Gon and Enforcer Brush Killer are effective undiluted for treating cut-stumps and available in retail garden stores (safe to surrounding plants).

Saplings. Apply a basal spray for trees up to 4 inches in diameter, using Garlon 4 as a 30-percent solution (7 pints per 3-gallon mix) in a labeled basal oil product, vegetable oil or mineral oil with a penetrant, or fuel oil or diesel fuel (where permitted).

Seedlings and saplings. Thoroughly wet all leaves with one of the following herbicides in water with a surfactant: a glyphosate herbicide as a 4-percent solution (1 pint per 3-gallon mix) whenever green foliage is present and when safety to surrounding plants is desired; or Arsenal AC* as a 1-percent solution (4 ounces per 3-gallon mix), or Arsenal PowerLine* as a 0.5-percent solution (2 ounces per 3-gallon mix).

---

* Nontarget plants may be killed or injured by root uptake.

Glossy Buckthorn

   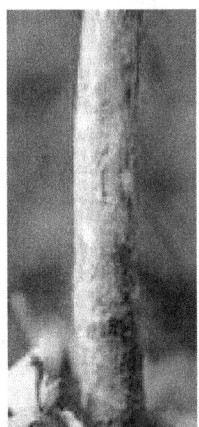

Leslie J. Mehrhoff

Glossy buckthorn (*Frangula alnus* Mill.) is a deciduous shrub or small tree that grows 6 to 24 feet (3 to 12 m) in height. It has many sprouts from the base, thornless stems up to 10 inches (25 cm) in diameter with glossy bark (thus the common name), and an oval, much-branched crown with many sprouts. Leaves appear early in spring and linger green into fall; leaves are dark glossy green and alternate with distinct parallel veins. Stemmed clusters of tiny, white trumpet flowers appear in summer and yield spherical, green berrylike fruit that turn red then black in the fall. Fruit consumed and spread by birds and mammals. Invades forest edges and understories and can form pure stands because seedlings can establish in shade. Resembles the native Carolina buckthorn [*F. caroliniana* (Walt.) Gray] that has finely serrated leaf margins and leaves that are three times as long as wide.

Management strategies:

- Bag and dispose of fruit in a dumpster or burn.
- Treatment combinations must be planned and enacted that safeguard adjoining shrubs and overstory trees.
- Treat when new plants are young to prevent seed formation.
- Manually pull new seedlings and tree wrench saplings when soil is moist, ensuring removal of all roots.
- Prescribed burning has limited application in most situations and can worsen infestations.

Recommended control procedures:

- When safety to surrounding vegetation is desired, thoroughly wet all leaves with a glyphosate herbicide or Garlon 3A as a 2- to 3-percent solution (8 to 12 ounces per 3-gallon mix) in water with a surfactant. Or if nontarget damage is not a concern, apply Arsenal AC* as a 0.25-percent solution (1 ounce per 3-gallon mix) or Arsenal PowerLine* as a 0.5-percent solution (2 ounces per 3-gallon mix). Apply July to October.
- For stems too tall for foliar sprays, cut large stems in winter at any time when the ground is not frozen and immediately treat the stump tops with one of the following herbicides: a glyphosate herbicide or Garlon 3A as a 25-percent solution (3 quarts per 3-gallon mix) or Garlon 3A as a 50-percent solution (6 quarts per 3-gallon mix) in water with a surfactant. Or when safety to surrounding plants is not a concern, Tordon RTU*. Roundup Pro, ORTHO Brush-B-Gon and Enforcer Brush Killer are effective undiluted for treating cut-stumps and available in retail garden stores (safe to surrounding plants). A subsequent foliar application may be required to control new seedlings and resprouts.
- For trees up to 4 inches in diameter, apply a basal spray of Garlon 4 as a 20-percent solution (5 pints per 3-gallon mix) in a labeled basal oil product, vegetable oil or mineral oil with a penetrant, fuel oil or diesel fuel (where permitted).

---

* Nontarget plants may be killed or injured by root uptake.

Paper Mulberry

Paper mulberry [*Broussonetia papifera* (L.) L'Hér. ex Vent.] is a traditional ornamental deciduous large shrub or tree with a round crown to 50 feet (15 m) in height and boles to 2 feet (0.6 m) in diameter, often appearing as shrub-forming thickets from root sprouts. Broad oval leaves that can be deeply lobed on rapidly growing stems are softly hairy on the lower surface (compared to the rough texture of other mulberry species) and scruffy above. Forms dense stands in fence rows, disturbed sites, and forest edges with shallow roots, and is prone to windthrow. Viable seed are rarely produced.

Management strategies:

- Do not plant. Remove prior plantings, and control sprouts. Bag and dispose of fruit in a dumpster or burn.
- Manually pull new seedlings and tree wrench saplings when soil is moist, ensuring removal of all roots.
- Burning treatments are suspected of having minimal topkill effect due to scant litter.
- Treatment combinations should be used that are appropriate for dense thickets with limited access. Access trails may need to be cut.

Recommended control procedures:

Large trees. Make stem injections at cut-spacing specified on the herbicide label using Garlon 3A as a 10-percent solution (1 quart per 3-gallon mix) in water or a 15-percent solution (58 ounces per 3-gallon mix) for larger trees, or cut large stems and immediately treat the stump tops with Garlon 3A as a 30-percent solution (7 pints per 3-gallon mix) in water with a surfactant. ORTHO Brush-B-Gon and Enforcer Brush Killer are effective undiluted for treating cut-stumps and available in retail garden stores (safe to surrounding plants).

Saplings. Apply basal sprays of Garlon 4 as a 20-percent solution (5 pints per 3-gallon mix) or when nontarget damage is not a concern, Stalker* as a 3-percent solution (12 ounces per 3-gallon mix) plus Garlon 4 as a 15-percent solution (3 pints per 3-gallon mix) in a labeled basal oil product, vegetable oil or mineral oil with a penetrant, or fuel oil or diesel fuel (where permitted).

Seedlings and saplings. Thoroughly wet all leaves with one of the following herbicides in water with a surfactant on young trees less than 10 feet tall (July to October): when safety to surrounding vegetation is desired, use Garlon 3A as a 2-percent solution (8 ounces per 3-gallon mix), Garlon 4 as a 0.5- to 2-percent solution (2 to 8 ounces per 3-gallon mix), or a glyphosate herbicide as a 3-percent solution (12 ounces per 3-gallon mix). If nontarget damage is not a concern, use Arsenal AC* as a 0.25-percent solution (1 ounce per 3-gallon mix) or Arsenal PowerLine* as a 0.5-percent solution (2 ounces per 3-gallon mix).

---

* Nontarget plants may be killed or injured by root uptake.

Princesstree, Paulownia

   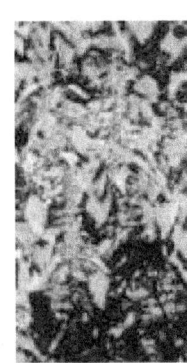 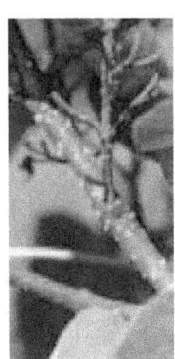 

Princesstree or paulownia [*Paulownia tomentosa* (Thunb.) Siebold & Zucc. ex Steud.] is a deciduous tree to 60 feet (18 m) tall with large heart-shaped leaves that are fuzzy hairy on both surfaces. Before leaves appear in spring, trees are covered with showy pale-violet flowers that yield persistent pecanlike capsules in clusters during fall and winter. Each capsule splits to release thousands of tiny winged seeds that are spread by wind, water, and gravity. Abundant flower buds are present on erect stalks over winter. Viable seed can be produced by 5- and 7-year-old plants. In the mountains, seed can be dispersed by wind up to 2 miles (3 km) away. Invades widely after fire, harvesting, and other disturbances. Forms colonies from prolific root sprouts. Still widely sold and planted as an "instant" shade tree as royal paulownia or royal empress.

Management strategies:
- Do not plant. Remove prior plantings, and control sprouts and seedlings. Bag and dispose of plants and capsules in a dumpster or burn.
- Minimize disturbance within miles of where this plant occurs.
- Treat when new plants are young to prevent seed formation.
- Cut when fruit are not present.
- Manually pull new seedlings and tree wrench saplings when soil is moist, ensuring removal of all roots.
- Burning treatments are suspected of having minimal topkill effect due to scant litter.

Recommended control procedures:
Large trees. Make stem injections using Arsenal AC* or when safety to surrounding vegetation is desired, Garlon 3A or a glyphosate herbicide in dilutions and cut-spacings specified on the herbicide label (anytime except March and April). For felled trees, apply these herbicides to stump tops immediately after cutting. Also, ORTHO Brush-B-Gon and Enforcer Brush Killer are effective undiluted for treating cut-stumps and available in retail garden stores (safe to surrounding plants).

Saplings. Apply a basal spray of Garlon 4 as a 20-percent solution (5 pints per 3-gallon mix) in a labeled basal oil product, or apply undiluted Pathfinder II when safety to surrounding vegetation is desired. Elsewhere, apply Stalker* as a 6- to 9-percent solution (1.5 to 2 pints per 3-gallon mix) in a labeled basal oil product, vegetable oil, kerosene, or diesel fuel (where permitted).

Resprouts and seedlings. Thoroughly wet all leaves with one of the following herbicides in water with a surfactant (July to October): Arsenal AC* as a 0.75-percent solution (3 ounces per 3-galllon mix); Arsenal PowerLine* as a 1.5-percent solution (6 ounces per 3-gallon mix); or when safety to surrounding vegetation is desired, a glyphosate herbicide, Garlon 3A, or Garlon 4 as a 2-percent solution (8 ounces per 3-gallon mix).

---
* Nontarget plants may be killed or injured by root uptake.

Russian Olive

Chris Evans

Patrick Breen

John Randall

Patrick Breen

Russian olive (*Elaeagnus angustifolia* L.) is a small thorny deciduous tree to 35 feet (10 m) tall that has microscopic silvery scales covering leaves, twigs, and fruits. Leaves are long and narrow with entire margins. Bark is fissured and reddish brown. Olivelike fruit are yellow (seldom red), appear in late summer to fall, and are spread by birds and mammals. Found as rare plants in city forests and emanating to nearby disturbed areas. Rare at present in the South while a widespread invasive tree elsewhere in the United States. Most often confused with the widely invasive autumn olive (*E. umbellata* Thunb.) that has silvery scaled leaves and twigs, red fruit that are only slightly scaly, and smooth bark.

Management strategies:

- Do not plant. Remove prior plantings, and control sprouts and seedlings. Bag and dispose of fruit in a dumpster or burn.
- Treat when new plants are young to prevent seed formation.
- Cut and bulldoze when fruit are not present.
- Manually pull new seedlings and tree wrench saplings when soil is moist, ensuring removal of all roots.
- Burning treatments are suspected of having minimal topkill effect due to scant litter.

Recommended control procedures:

Trees. Make stem injections using Arsenal AC* or Garlon 3A in dilutions and cut-spacings specified on the herbicide label (anytime except March and April). For felled trees, apply the herbicides to stump tops immediately after cutting. ORTHO Brush-B-Gon and Enforcer Brush Killer are effective undiluted for treating cut-stumps and available in retail garden stores (safe to surrounding plants).

Saplings. When safety to surrounding vegetation is desired, apply a basal spray to young bark using either Garlon 4 as a 20-percent solution (5 pints per 3-gallon mix) in a labeled basal oil product, vegetable oil or mineral oil with a penetrant, or fuel oil or diesel fuel (where permitted); or undiluted Pathfinder II. Or when safety to surrounding vegetation is not a concern, apply Stalker* as a 6- to 9-percent solution (1.5 to 2 pints per 3-gallon mix) in a labeled basal oil product, vegetable oil, kerosene, or diesel fuel (where permitted).

Seedlings and saplings. Thoroughly wet all leaves with one of the following herbicides in water with a surfactant (July to October): Arsenal AC* as a 0.75-percent solution in water (3 ounces per 3-gallon mix) or Arsenal PowerLine* as a 1.5-percent solution (6 ounces per 3-gallon mix). Or when safety to surrounding vegetation is desired, use a glyphosate herbicide, Garlon 3A, or Garlon 4 as a 2-percent solution in water (8 ounces per 3-gallon mix). Use any of these three mixtures for directed spray treatments that have limited or no soil activity.

---

* Nontarget plants may be killed or injured by root uptake.

Silktree, Mimosa

Silktree or mimosa (*Albizia julibrissin* Durazz.) is a small legume tree 10 to 50 feet (3 to 15 m) tall that reproduces by abundant seeds and root sprouts. Traditionally planted as an ornamental owing to abundant showy pink and white flowers in spring and throughout summer that yield profuse dangling flat pods that are often retained during winter. It has feathery deciduous leaves and smooth light-brown bark. Seedpods float to spread along waterways and ditches, while seed remain viable for many years.

Management strategies:
- Do not plant. Remove prior plantings, and control sprouts and seedlings. Bag and dispose of seed pods in a dumpster or burn.
- Minimize disturbance where this plant occurs.
- Treat when new plants are young to prevent seed formation.
- Cut and bulldoze when seed are not present.
- Manually pull new seedlings and tree wrench saplings when soil is moist, ensuring removal of all roots.
- Burning treatments are suspected of having minimal topkill effect due to scant litter.

Recommended control procedures:
Trees. Make stem injections using Arsenal AC* or when safety to surrounding vegetation is desired, Garlon 3A in dilutions as specified on the herbicide label (anytime except March and April). For felled trees, apply the herbicides to stump tops immediately after cutting. ORTHO Brush-B-Gon and Enforcer Brush Killer are effective undiluted for treating cut-stumps and available in retail garden stores (safe to surrounding plants).

Saplings. Apply a basal spray to young bark using Garlon 4 as a 20-percent solution (5 pints per 3-gallon mix) in a labeled basal oil product, vegetable oil or mineral oil with a penetrant, or fuel oil or diesel fuel (where permitted); or undiluted Pathfinder II. Elsewhere, apply Stalker* as a 6- to 9-percent solution (1.5 to 2 pints per 3-gallon mix) in a labeled basal oil product, vegetable oil, kerosene, or diesel fuel (where permitted).

Resprouts and seedlings. Thoroughly wet all leaves with one of the following herbicides in water with a surfactant:
- From June to August, either Escort XP* at 1 ounce per acre (0.2 ounces per 3-gallon mix) plus a glyphosate herbicide as a 2-percent solution addition (8 ounces per 3-gallon mix) or Milestone VM* at 6 to 9 pints per acre (1.5 to 3 pints per 3-gallon mix and 10 gallons per acre).
- From July to September, Transline* [†] as a 0.25-percent solution plus Garlon 3A as a 4-percent solution (1 ounce plus 1 pint per 3-gallon mix).

---

* Nontarget plants may be killed or injured by root uptake.

[†] Transline controls a narrow spectrum of plant species.

Tallowtree, Popcorntree

 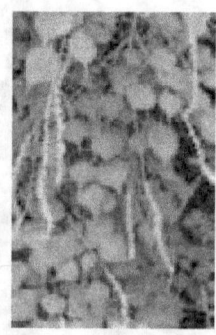 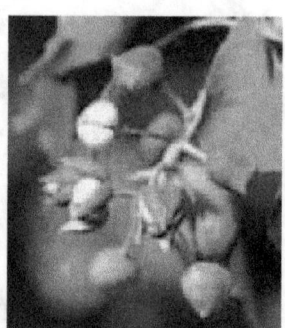  

Tallowtree or popcorntree [*Triadica sebifera* (L.) Small], formerly [*Sapium sebiferum* (L.) Roxb.] is a deciduous tree growing to 60 feet (18 m) tall that can form pure stands, especially in wet prairies. Leaves are broadly ovate to diamond-shaped and turn bright yellow and scarlet in the fall. Abundant bundles of white waxy popcorn-like seeds appear on branchlets in the fall also. Seeds, high in fat and protein, are consumed and spread by birds and mammals. Saplings as young as 3 years can produce viable seed and remain reproductive for 100 years to produce 100,000 seeds per year. Infestations intensify by prolific surface root sprouts. Seed viability in the soil is 2 to 7 years.

Management strategies:

- Do not plant. Remove prior plantings, and control sprouts and seedlings. Bag and dispose of fruit in a dumpster or burn.
- Tallowtree litter mulch inhibits its own seed germination as well as native seeds.
- Minimize disturbance within miles of where this plant occurs, and anticipate wider occupation when plants are present before disturbance.
- High-priority sites to monitor and treat are by water.
- Treat when new plants are young to prevent seed formation.
- Cut, bulldoze, and mulch when fruit are not present.
- Manually pull new seedlings and tree wrench saplings when soil is moist, ensuring removal of all roots.
- Burning treatments intensify infestations and should not be used.

Recommended control procedures:

Large trees. Make stem injections using dilutions and cut-spacings specified on the herbicide label (anytime except March and April) with Arsenal AC*, Clearcast*, or Habitat* herbicide in aquatic situations; or when safety to surrounding vegetation is desired, inject Garlon 3A or a glyphosate herbicide.

- For felled trees and cut saplings, apply a herbicide to stump tops and sides immediately after cutting using Garlon 4 as a 10-percent solution in a basal oil (1 quart per 3-gallon mix) when stumps are less than 6 inches in diameter and a 20-percent solution (2 quarts per 3-gallon mix) on larger stumps, or apply Garlon 3A or a glyphosate herbicide mixed in water as a 20-percent solution (2 quarts per 3-gallon mix) on all sizes of stumps. ORTHO Brush-B-Gon and Enforcer Brush Killer are effective undiluted for treating cut-stumps and available in retail garden stores (safe to surrounding plants). Follow the label directions.
- For treatment of extensive infestations in forest situations, apply Velpar L* to the soil surface within 3 feet of the stem (one squirt per 1-inch stem diameter) or in a grid pattern at spacings specified on the herbicide label, or Clearcast* as an aerial spray, which has safety to many hardwoods, at 48 ounces per acre.

Saplings. Apply Garlon 4 as a 15-percent solution (58 ounces per 3-gallon mix) in a labeled basal oil product, vegetable oil or mineral oil with a penetrant, or fuel oil or diesel fuel (where permitted); undiluted Pathfinder II when safety to surrounding vegetation is desired; or elsewhere, Stalker* as a 6- to 9-percent solution (1.5 to 2 pints per 3-gallon mix) in a labeled basal oil product, vegetable oil or mineral oil with a penetrant, or fuel oil or diesel fuel (where permitted) to young bark as a basal spray.

Seedlings and saplings. Thoroughly wet all leaves with one of the following herbicides in water with a surfactant (July to October): Arsenal AC* as a 0.75-percent solution (3 ounces per 3-gallon mix); Arsenal PowerLine* as a 1.5-percent solution (6 ounces per 3-gallon mix); Krenite S as a 20-percent solution (5 pints per 3-gallon mix); Clearcast* as a 2-percent solution (8 ounces per 3-gallon mix); or when safety to surrounding vegetation is desired, Garlon 4 as a 2-percent solution (8 ounces per 3-gallon mix).

---

* Nontarget plants may be killed or injured by root uptake.

Tree-of-Heaven

    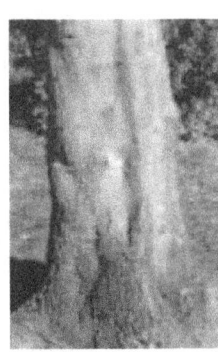

Tree-of-heaven or ailanthus [*Ailanthus altissima* (Mill.) Swingle] is a shallow-rooted deciduous tree to 80 feet (25 m) tall with long pinnately compound leaves having two circular glands under small lobes on leaflet bases. Large terminal clusters of greenish flowers in early summer yield persistent clusters of wing-shaped fruit with twisted tips on female trees. Light-green seeds in midsummer are capable of germination. Viable seed are produced by 2- to 3-year-old plants, and a mature tree can produce 300,000 seeds per year. Seed can be blown up to 330 feet (100 m) from parent. Root sprouts will appear after the main stem is deadened, and root segments left in soil after pulling treatments will sprout. Sprouts can grow 10 to 14 feet (3 to 4 m) tall the first year. This vigorous growth can continue for 4 or more years.

Management strategies:

- Do not plant. Remove prior plantings, and control sprouts and seedlings. Bag and dispose of fruit in a dumpster or burn.
- Target female seed-producing plants.
- Minimize disturbance within miles of where this plant occurs, and anticipate wider occupation when plants are present before disturbance.
- Treat when new plants are young to prevent seed formation.
- Cutting and pulling treatments result in abundant surface root sprouts and should not be used without herbicide treatments.
- Burning treatments are suspected of having minimal topkill effect due to scant litter.

Recommended control procedures:

Large trees. Make stem injections and then apply Garlon 3A when safety to surrounding vegetation is desired, or Pathway* or Arsenal AC* in dilutions and cut-spacings specified on the herbicide label (midsummer best, late winter somewhat less effective). For felled trees, apply the herbicides to stem and stump tops immediately after cutting. Also, ORTHO Brush-B-Gon and Enforcer Brush Killer are effective undiluted for treating cut-stumps and available in retail garden stores (safe to surrounding plants).

Saplings. Apply as basal sprays in mixed in a labeled basal oil product, vegetable oil or mineral oil with a penetrant, or fuel oil or diesel fuel (where permitted) using Garlon 4 as a 20-percent solution (5 pints per 3-gallon mix) when safety to surrounding vegetation is desired; or Stalker* as a 6- to 9-percent solution (1.5 to 2 pints per 3-gallon mix).

Seedlings and saplings. Thoroughly wet all leaves with one of the following herbicides in water with a surfactant (July to October): Arsenal AC* as a 0.75-percent solution (3 ounces per 3-gallon mix); Arsenal PowerLine* as a 1.5-percent solution (6 ounces per 3-gallon mix); Krenite S as a 15-percent solution (58 ounces per 3-gallon mix); Escort XP* at 1 ounce per acre; or when safety to surrounding vegetation is desired, Garlon 4 as a 1- to 2-percent solution (4 to 8 ounces per 3-gallon mix) or Garlon 3A as a 2-percent solution (8 ounces per 3-gallon mix).

---

* Nontarget plants may be killed or injured by root uptake.

Trifoliate, Hardy Orange

Trifoliate or hardy orange [*Poncirus trifoliata* (L.) Raf.] is a deciduous, small tree or shrub to 20 feet (6 m) in height and with tufts of trifoliate (three-leaflet) leaves on densely packed thorny stems. White flowers cover plants in early spring to yield abundant small, fuzzy green orangelike fruit that turn yellow in fall. Many sprouts occur around stems but not from roots. Species spreads by prolific animal-dispersed seeds and colonizes by basal sprouts.

Management strategies:
- Do not plant. Remove prior plantings, and control sprouts and seedlings. Bag and dispose of fruit in a dumpster or burn.
- Treat when new plants are young to prevent seed formation.
- Cut and bulldoze when fruit are not present.
- Anticipate wider occupation when plants are present before disturbance.
- Cutting, tree injection, manual pulling, and tree wrenching are hindered by dense thorny branches and basal sprouts so use eye protection.
- Manually pull new seedlings and tree wrench saplings when soil is moist, ensuring removal of all roots.
- Burning treatments are suspected of having minimal topkill effect due to scant litter.
- Treatment combinations should be used that are appropriate for dense thickets with limited access. Access trails may need to be cut.

Recommended control procedures:
Large trees and saplings. Cut and immediately treat the stump tops with one of the following herbicides: a glyphosate herbicide or Garlon 3A as a 25-percent solution (3 quarts per 1-gallon mix). ORTHO Brush-B-Gon and Enforcer Brush Killer are effective undiluted for treating cut-stumps and available in retail garden stores (safe to surrounding plants). A subsequent foliar application may be required to control new seedlings and resprouts.

Saplings. When safety to surrounding vegetation is desired, apply a basal spray of either Pathfinder II undiluted or Garlon 4 as a 20-percent solution (5 pints per 3-gallon mix) in a labeled basal oil product, vegetable oil or mineral oil with a penetrant, or fuel oil or diesel fuel (where permitted). Elsewhere, apply Stalker* as a 6- to 9-percent solution (1.5 to 2 pints per 3-gallon mix) in a labeled basal oil product, vegetable oil or mineral oil with a penetrant, or fuel oil or diesel fuel (where permitted).

Seedlings. When safety to surrounding vegetation is desired, thoroughly wet all leaves with a glyphosate herbicide or Garlon 3A as a 4-percent solution (1 pint per 3-gallon mix) in water with a surfactant; or if nontarget damage is not a concern, apply Arsenal AC* as a 0.5-percent solution (2 ounces per 3-gallon mix).

---

* Nontarget plants may be killed or injured by root uptake.

Tungoil Tree

    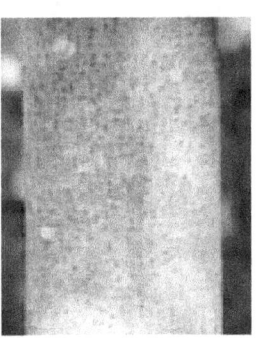

Tungoil tree [*Vernicia fordii* (Hemsl.) Airy-Shaw] is a deciduous tree that grows rapidly in moist and well-drained soils, forming dense stands. Trees grow to 40 feet (12 m) in height and have rounded crowns with many alternate branches and basal sprouts. Leaves are heart-shaped, some with rounded sinuses (mittenlike), and long petioles with a pair of conspicuous dark glands at the juncture with the blade. Sap is milky white. Clusters of showy, white, trumpet flowers with orange throats in early spring yield large spherical "nuts" in the fall. Viable seed can be produced at 3 years. Still sparingly planted as an ornamental.

Management strategies:

- Do not plant. Remove prior plantings, and control sprouts and seedlings. Bag and dispose of fruit in a dumpster or burn.
- Treat when new plants are young to prevent seed formation.
- Cut, mulch, and bulldoze when fruit are not present.
- Manually pull new seedlings and tree wrench saplings when soil is moist, ensuring removal of all roots.
- Burning treatments are suspected of having minimal topkill effect due to scant litter.

Recommended control procedures:

Large trees and saplings. Make stem injections using undiluted Garlon 3A (June through September) when safety to surrounding vegetation is desired or Vanquish* as a 75-percent solution (9 quarts per 3-gallon mix) with water (June through October) in cut-spacings specified on the herbicide label. For stems too tall for foliar sprays, cut and immediately treat the stump tops with one of the following herbicides: Garlon 4 as a 25- to 50-percent solution (3 to 6 quarts per 3-gallon mix) or Garlon 3A as a 30-percent solution (7 pints per 3-gallon mix). ORTHO Brush-B-Gon and Enforcer Brush Killer are effective undiluted for treating cut-stumps and available in retail garden stores (safe to surrounding plants).

Saplings. When safety to surrounding vegetation is desired, apply a basal spray of Pathfinder II undiluted. Otherwise, use Garlon 4 as a 20-percent solution (5 pints per 3-gallon mix) in a labeled basal oil product, vegetable oil or mineral oil with a penetrant, or fuel oil or diesel fuel (where permitted). Elsewhere, apply Stalker* as a 6- to 9-percent solution (1.5 to 2 pints per 3-gallon mix) in a labeled basal oil product, vegetable oil or mineral oil with a penetrant, or fuel oil or diesel fuel (where permitted).

Seedlings and saplings. Wet all leaves on young trees < 10 feet (3 m) tall using one of the following herbicides in water with a surfactant: Garlon 3A as a 2-percent solution (8 ounces per 3-gallon mix), a glyphosate herbicide as a 2- to 3-percent solution (8 to 12 ounces per 3-gallon mix) when safety to surrounding vegetation is desired, Chopper Gen2* as a 1-percent solution (4 ounces per 3-gallon mix), or Arsenal AC* as a 0.5-percent solution (2 ounces per 3-gallon mix).

* Nontarget plants may be killed or injured by root uptake.

Invasive Shrubs

Invasive shrubs often occur with invasive tree species and present similar problems. Herbicide control options are similar to those for trees, with the exception that foliar sprays can be used more often. All are shade tolerant with bird-dispersed seeds, resulting in scattered plants under existing forest canopies, which require additional surveillance within the interior of forest stands.

Autumn Olive

PA Dept. Cons. Nat. Res. - Forestry Archive

Autumn olive (*Elaeagnus umbellata* Thunb.) is a tardily deciduous bushy leafy shrub, 3 to 20 feet (1 to 6 m) in height, with scattered thorny branches. It has alternate leaves that are green above and silvery scaly beneath, with many red berries in fall having silvery scales. Species spreads by bird- and mammal-dispersed seeds. Often planted for surface-mine reclamation and wildlife food plots and escapes to forest edges and open forests.

Management strategies:
- Do not plant. Remove prior plantings, and control sprouts and seedlings. Bag and dispose of fruit in a dumpster or burn.
- Treat when new plants are young to prevent seed formation.
- Cut and bulldoze when fruit are not present.
- Minimize disturbance within miles of where this plant occurs, and anticipate wider occupation when plants are present before disturbance.
- Cutting and basal treatments are hindered by multiple thorny sprouts and eye protection should be used.
- Manually pull new seedlings and tree wrench saplings when soil is moist, ensuring removal of all roots.
- Burning treatments are suspected of having minimal topkill effect due to scant litter.
- Autumn olive seedlings are readily eaten by goats and sheep. Goats can deaden saplings by striping the bark and bending them over to eat the foliage.

Recommended control procedures:
- Thoroughly wet all leaves with Arsenal AC* or Vanquish* as a 1-percent solution in water (4 ounces per 3-gallon mix) with a surfactant (April to October). Or when safety to surrounding vegetation is desired, use Garlon 3A as a 2 percent solution (8 ounces per 3-gallon mix).
- For stems too tall for foliar sprays, apply (January to February or May to October) a basal spray using Garlon 4 as a 20-percent solution (5 pints per 3-gallon mix) in a labeled basal oil product, vegetable oil or mineral oil with a penetrant, or fuel oil or diesel fuel (where permitted), or undiluted Pathfinder II when safety to surrounding vegetation is desired. Elsewhere, apply Stalker* as a 6-percent solution (1.5 pints per 3-gallon mix) in a labeled basal oil product, vegetable oil or mineral oil with a penetrant, or fuel oil or diesel fuel (where permitted) to young stems. Or cut larger stems and immediately treat the stump tops with one of the following herbicides in water with a surfactant: Arsenal AC* as a 5-percent solution (20 ounces per 3-gallon mix); or when safety to surrounding vegetation is desired, a glyphosate herbicide as a 20-percent solution (5 pints per 3-gallon mix). ORTHO Brush-B-Gon and Enforcer Brush Killer are effective undiluted for treating cut-stumps and available in retail garden stores (safe to surrounding plants).

---

* Nontarget plants may be killed or injured by root uptake.

Bush Honeysuckles

   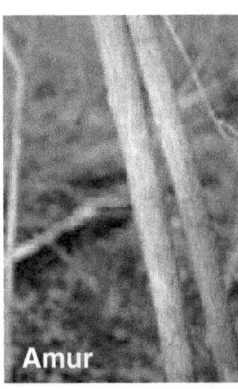

Amur honeysuckle [*Lonicera maackii* (Rupr.) Herder], Morrow's honeysuckle (*L. morrowii* Gray), Tatarian honeysuckle (*L. tatarica* L.), sweet breath of spring (*L. fragrantissima* Lindl. & Paxton), and Bell's honeysuckle (*Lonicera ×bella* Zabel [morrowii × tatarica]) are all tardily deciduous, upright to arching-branched shrubs. All are multiple stemmed with dark green oval-to-oblong distinctly opposite leaves that appear early. Fragrant showy tubular and five-lipped white-to-pink or yellow paired flowers similar to Japanese honeysuckle (*L. japonica* L.) appear from May to June. Abundant paired berries in leaf axils are red to orange during winter and are spread by birds and mammals. Seeds are long lived in the soil. Infestations intensify by root sprouts.

Management strategies:
- Do not plant. Remove prior plantings, and control sprouts and seedlings. Bag and dispose of fruit in a dumpster or burn.
- Minimize disturbance within miles of where these plants occur, and anticipate wider occupation when plants are present before disturbance.
- Treat new plants when young to prevent seed formation.
- Repeated cutting to prevent fruiting once a year in forests will diminish stands. Cut only when fruit are not present.
- Manual pulling, tree wrenching, and grubbing with a pick mattock can control small plants and small populations when roots are removed; these strategies are easiest when soil is moist. Soils should be tamped down to discourage further invasion.
- Burning treatments are most effective in spring for seedling kill and topkill. Repeat for suppression.
- Bush honeysuckles are not readily eaten by goats, deer, or sheep, while high deer densities unless controlled will slow revegetation by native plants.
- Treatment access can be limited by dense growth and will warrant trail cutting.

Recommended control procedures:
- Thoroughly wet all leaves with glyphosate herbicide, Garlon 3A, or Garlon 4 as a 4-percent solution in water (1 pint per 3-gallon mix) with a surfactant (April to October); or when leaves turn yellow, increase the strength of the Garlon 4 application to a 6-percent solution (20 ounces per 3-gallon mix). Other alternatives include: Garlon 4 as a 20-percent solution (5 pints per 3-gallon) mix in a labeled basal oil product, vegetable oil or mineral oil with a penetrant, or fuel oil or diesel fuel (where permitted); or undiluted Pathfinder II* applied to young bark as a basal spray to all stems in a clump (winter applications recommended).
- For stems too tall for foliar sprays, cut large stems and saplings and immediately treat the stump tops with one of the following herbicides when safety to surrounding vegetation is desired: a glyphosate herbicide, Garlon 3A as a 20-percent solution (5 pints per 3-gallon mix), or undiluted Pathfinder II. ORTHO Brush-B-Gon and Enforcer Brush Killer are effective undiluted for treating cut-stumps and available in retail garden stores (safe to surrounding plants). Elsewhere, apply Pathway* undiluted in summer or fall. Treating in the spring will result in significantly lower control, especially when using a glyphosate herbicide.
- For large stems, make stem injections using Arsenal AC* or when safety to surrounding vegetation is desired, Garlon 3A or a glyphosate herbicide using dilutions and cut-spacings specified on the herbicide label (anytime except March and April). An EZ-Ject tree injector can help to reach the lower part of the main stem; otherwise, every branching trunk must be hack-and-squirt injected.

---

* Nontarget plants may be killed or injured by root uptake.

Chinese/European/Border/California Privets

Chinese privet | Chinese privet | Chinese privet | Chinese privet | Chinese privet

Chinese (*Ligustrum sinense* Lour.), European (*L. vulgare* L.), border (*L. obtusifolium* Siebold & Zucc.), and California privets (*L. ovalifolium* Hassk.) are shrubs with thin opposite leaves, semievergreen to evergreen, and thicket forming to 30 feet (9 m) in height. All have multiple leaning-to-arching stems with long leafy branches. Chinese privet is one of the most widely spread invasive plants in the South, while the other three are uncommon. All have showy clusters of small white flowers in spring that yield abundant clusters of small ovoid, dark purple berries during fall and winter. Aggressive and troublesome invasives, often forming dense thickets, particularly in bottomland forests and along fencerows. Shade tolerant. Colonize by root sprouts and spread widely by abundant bird- and animal-dispersed seeds. Seeds thought to be viable for only 1 year. Many shallow surface roots that sprout when parent tree is topkilled. Still being produced, sold, and planted as ornamentals.

Management strategies:

- Do not plant. Remove prior plantings, and control sprouts and seedlings. Bag and dispose of fruit in a dumpster or burn.
- Minimize disturbance within miles of where these plants occur, and anticipate wider occupation if plants are present before disturbance.
- Treat when new plants are young to prevent seed formation.
- Cut and bulldoze when fruit are not present.
- Manually pull new seedlings and tree wrench saplings when soil is moist, ensuring removal of all roots.
- Burns hot when green to topkill small to medium-sized stems.
- Readily eaten by goats, sheep, and deer when reachable.

Recommended control procedures:

- Thoroughly wet all leaves with one of the following herbicides in water with a surfactant: a glyphosate herbicide as a 3-percent solution (12 ounces per 3-gallon mix) when safety to surrounding vegetation is desired, or elsewhere, Arsenal AC* as a 1-percent solution (4 ounces per 3-gallon mix). Backpack mist blowers can broadcast glyphosate as a 3-percent solution (12 ounces per 3-gallon mix) or Escort XP* at 1 ounce per acre (0.2 dry ounces per 3-gallon mix and 10 gallons per acre) during winter for safety to dormant hardwoods. Summer applications of glyphosate may not be as effective as other times and require a higher percent solution. The best time period for Arsenal AC* and Escort XP* is summer to fall.
- For stems too tall for foliar sprays and when safety to surrounding vegetation is desired, apply a basal spray of Garlon 4 as a 20-percent solution (5 pints per 3-gallon mix) in a labeled basal oil product, vegetable oil or mineral oil with a penetrant, or fuel oil or diesel fuel (where permitted); or undiluted Pathfinder II. Elsewhere, apply Stalker* as a 6- to 9-percent solution (1.5 to 2 pints per 3-gallon mix) in a labeled basal oil product, vegetable oil or mineral oil with a penetrant, or fuel oil or diesel fuel (where permitted) to young bark as a basal spray making certain to treat all stems in a clump; or cut and immediately treat the stump tops with Arsenal AC* as a 5-percent solution (20 ounces per 3-gallon mix) or Velpar L* as a 10-percent solution in water (1 quart per 3-gallon mix) with a surfactant. When safety to surrounding vegetation is desired, immediately treat stump tops and sides with Garlon 3A or with a glyphosate herbicide as a 20-percent solution (5 pints per 3-gallon mix) in water with a surfactant. ORTHO Brush-B-Gon and Enforcer Brush Killer are effective undiluted for treating cut-stumps and available in retail garden stores (safe to surrounding plants).
- For large stems, make stem injections using Arsenal AC* or when safety to surrounding vegetation is desired, Garlon 3A or a glyphosate herbicide using dilutions and cut-spacings specified on the herbicide label (anytime except March and April). An EZ-Ject tree injector can help to reach the lower part of the main stem; otherwise, every branching trunk must be hack-and-squirt injected.

---

* Nontarget plants may be killed or injured by root uptake.

Hen's Eyes, Coral Ardisia

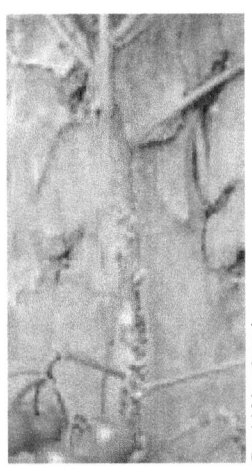

Hen's eyes or coral ardisia (*Ardisia crenata* Sims) is an evergreen erect shrub, 2 to 6 feet (0.6 to 1.8 m) in height with short stems or multistemmed bushy clumps. The species is distinguished by shiny green leaves with distinct thickened, wavy margins. Drooping white to pink axillary flowers appear all summer to yield dangling, bright red berries fall and through winter. Spreads and colonizes by animal-dispersed seed to form dense infestations. Plants produce fruit within 2 years.

Management strategies:
- Do not plant. Remove prior plantings, and control sprouts and seedlings. Bag and dispose of fruit in a dumpster or burn.
- Treat when new plants are young to prevent seed formation.
- Cut, mulch, or bulldoze when fruit are not present.
- Minimize disturbance within miles of where this plant occurs, and anticipate wider occupation when plants are present before disturbance.
- Manually pull new seedlings and tree wrench saplings when soil is moist, ensuring removal of all roots.
- Burning treatments are suspected of having minimal effect due to scant litter.

Recommended control procedures:
- In fall, apply a basal spray of Garlon 4 as a 20-percent solution (5 pints per 3-gallon mix) in a labeled basal oil product, vegetable oil or mineral oil with a penetrant, or fuel oil or diesel fuel (where permitted).
- For stems too tall for foliar sprays, cut large stems and immediately treat the stump tops with Garlon 4 as a 20- to 25-percent solution (5 to 6 pints per 3-gallon mix). ORTHO Brush-B-Gon and Enforcer Brush Killer are effective undiluted for treating cut-stumps and available in retail garden stores (safe to surrounding plants).
- Thoroughly wet all leaves with one of the following herbicides in water with a surfactant: a glyphosate herbicide or Garlon 4 as a 5-percent solution (20 ounces per 3-gallon mix).

Japanese/Glossy Privet

Japanese privet (*Ligustrum japonicum* Thunb.) and glossy privet (*L. lucidum* W.T. Aiton) are evergreen shrubs to 35 feet (10 m) in height, with upward spreading canopies. They have thick leathery opposite leaves 2 to 4 inches (5 to 10 cm) long that are glossy, and stems are hairless. In spring, terminal panicles of small showy white flowers yield clusters of small rounded green-to-purple fruit in fall that often persist through winter into spring. These invade both lowland and upland habitats, but usually are more prevalent in lowlands and are shade tolerant. They colonize by root sprouts and spread widely by abundant bird- and animal-dispersed seeds. Seeds thought to be viable for only 1 year. The abundant shallow surface roots sprout when a parent tree is topkilled. Still being sold and planted as ornamentals.

Management strategies:
- Do not plant. Remove prior plantings, and control sprouts and seedlings. Bag and dispose of fruit in a dumpster or burn.
- Treat when new plants are young to prevent seed formation.
- Cut, mulch, and bulldoze when fruit are not present.
- Minimize disturbance within miles of where these plants occur, and anticipate wider occupation if plants are present before disturbance.
- Manually pull and tree wrench when soil is moist, ensuring removal of all roots.
- These species burn hot to topkill small to medium-sized stems.
- Readily eaten by goats and sheep.

Recommended control procedures:
- For large stems, make stem injections in dilutions and cut-spacings specified on the herbicide label using Arsenal AC*, or when safety to surrounding vegetation is desired, Garlon 3A or a glyphosate herbicide (anytime except March and April). An EZ-Ject tree injector can help to reach the lower part of the main stem; otherwise, every branching trunk must be hack-and-squirt injected.
- Thoroughly wet all leaves with one of the following herbicides in water with a surfactant: Arsenal AC* as a 1-percent solution (4 ounces per 3-gallon mix); or when safety to surrounding vegetation is desired, Garlon 4 as a 3-percent solution (12 ounces per 3-gallon mix) or a glyphosate herbicide as a 3-percent solution (12 ounces per 3-gallon mix). The best time for applications is when new growth appears, while other times have not been tested.
- For stems too tall for foliar sprays, apply basal sprays in a labeled basal oil product, vegetable oil or mineral oil with a penetrant, or fuel oil or diesel fuel (where permitted); when safety to surrounding vegetation is desired, Garlon 4 as a 20-percent solution (5 pints per 3-gallon mix) or undiluted Pathfinder II. Elsewhere, apply Stalker* as a 6- to 9-percent solution (1.5 to 2 pints per 3-gallon mix) in a labeled basal oil product, vegetable oil or mineral oil with a penetrant, or where permitted, fuel oil or diesel fuel (January to February or May to October).
- Cut large stems and immediately treat the stump tops with Arsenal AC* as a 5-percent solution (20 ounces per 3-gallon mix) or Velpar L* as a 10-percent solution (1 quart per 3-gallon mix) in water with a surfactant. When safety to surrounding vegetation is desired, immediately treat cut stems and stump tops with a glyphosate herbicide or Garlon 3A as a 20-percent solution in water (5 pints per 3-gallon mix) with a surfactant. ORTHO Brush-B-Gon and Enforcer Brush Killer are effective undiluted for treating cut-stumps and available in retail garden stores (safe to surrounding plants).

---

* Nontarget plants may be killed or injured by root uptake.

Japanese Barberry

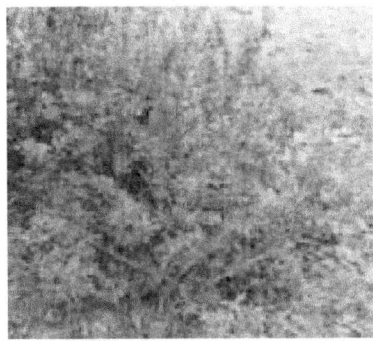

Leslie Mehrhoff

Japanese barberry (*Berberis thunbergii* DC.) is a tardily deciduous, compact, and spreading shrub 2 to 4 feet (60 to 120 cm) in height and slightly wider, occasionally 6 to 8 feet (1.8 to 3 m) high. Leaves are alternate in tight clusters, spatulate (paddle shaped) with entire margins and bases narrowing to the stem. Forms dense infestations under forest canopies but prefers partial shade of edges to exclude other plants. Infestations intensify by root sprouts and rooting of drooping stems. Seeds remain viable in the soil for up to 10 years. Application of herbicides early in the season before native vegetation has matured may minimize nontarget impacts. However, application in late summer during fruiting may be most effective. Resembles both the nonnative invasive common or European barberry (*B. vulgaris* L.) and the native American barberry (*B. canadensis* Mill.), while both have finely bristled leaf margins. Also resembles a rare escaped wintergreen barberry (*B. julianae* C.K. Schneid.) in the mountains that has leathery, evergreen leaves.

Management strategies:
- Do not plant. Remove prior plantings, and control sprouts and seedlings. Bag and dispose of fruit in a dumpster or burn.
- Treat when new plants are young to prevent seed formation.
- Cut or mulch when fruit are not present.
- Minimize disturbance within miles of where this plant occurs, and anticipate wider occupation when plants are present before disturbance.
- Manually pull and tree wrench when soil is moist, ensuring removal of all roots.
- Burns hot when green to topkill small to medium-sized stems.
- Readily eaten by goats and sheep.

Recommended control procedures:
- Thoroughly wet all leaves with a glyphosate herbicide or Garlon 3A as a 2-percent solution (8 ounces per 3-gallon mix) in water with a surfactant.
- Cut large stems and immediately treat with one of the following herbicides: a glyphosate herbicide or Garlon 3A as a 25-percent solution (3 quarts per 3-gallon mix). ORTHO Brush-B-Gon and Enforcer Brush Killer are effective undiluted for treating cut-stumps and available in retail garden stores (safe to surrounding plants).
- Subsequent foliar applications may be required to control new seedlings and resprouts.

Japanese Knotweed

Steven T. Manning

Japanese knotweed (*Polygonum cuspidatum* Siebold & Zucc.) is a tall perennial, canelike shrub 3 to 12 feet (1 to 3.5 m) in height, freely branching in dense, often clonal infestations. Hollow-jointed, reddish stems like bamboo survive only one season while rhizomes survive decades. Alternate leaves appear in spring on new sprouts, ovate with pointed tips and flat bases. In late summer, sprays of tiny white flowers emerge along stalks at leaf axils that yield abundant tiny winged seeds with highly variable viability. Dead tops remain standing during winter. Japanese knotweed spreads along streams by stem and rhizome fragments, and rare seeds to dominate extensive riparian habitat. Also, spreads along highways and roads by similar means through maintenance mowing.

Management strategies:

- Do not plant. Remove prior plantings, and control sprouts and seedlings. Bag and dispose of fruit in a dumpster or burn.
- Minimize disturbance within miles of where this plant occurs, and anticipate wider occupation when plants are present before disturbance.
- Repeated cutting and pulling will not control this species unless young.
- Burns hot in dormant season to clear tops with rhizomes remaining.

Recommended control procedures:

- Thoroughly wet all leaves with one of the following herbicides in water with a surfactant: Garlon 3A (or aquatic Renovate) as a 2-percent solution (8 ounces per 3-gallon mix); better results may occur from a mix of Garlon 3A as a 1-percent solution (4 ounces per 3-gallon mix) and a glyphosate herbicide (Rodeo for aquatic sites) as a 2-percent solution (8 ounces per 3-gallon mix). Fall applications are most effective while seed production where it occurs can be stopped by earlier treatments.
- On terrestrial sites when safety to nontarget vegetation is not a concern, thoroughly wet all leaves with Arsenal AC[*] as a 0.25-percent solution (1 ounce per 3-gallon mix), Arsenal PowerLine[*] as a 0.5-percent solution (2 ounces per 3-gallon mix), Tordon 101[*][‡] as a 4-percent solution (1 pint per 3-gallon mix), or Tordon K[*][‡] as a 2-percent solution (8 ounces per 3-gallon mix).
- On aquatic sites, thoroughly wet all leaves at flower plume stage with Habitat[*] as a 1-percent solution (4 ounces per 3-gallon mix) mixed with an aquatic surfactant.
- For stems too tall for foliar sprays, cut large stems and immediately treat the stump tops with one of the following herbicides: a glyphosate herbicide or Garlon 3A as a 25-percent solution (3 quarts per 3-gallon mix). ORTHO Brush-B-Gon and Enforcer Brush Killer are effective undiluted for treating cut-stumps and available in retail garden stores (safe to surrounding plants). A subsequent foliar application of glyphosate will be required to control new seedlings and resprouts.

---

[*] Nontarget plants may be killed or injured by root uptake.

[‡] When using Tordon herbicides, rainfall must occur within 6 days after application for needed soil activation. Tordon herbicides are restricted use pesticides.

Japanese Meadowsweet

Great Smoky Mtns. NP Res. Mgmt. Archive

Japanese meadowsweet or Japanese spiraea (*Spiraea japonica* L.f.) is a deciduous erect shrub to 6 feet (1.8 m) high with multiple stems and alternate branches, slender and brown, intertwining or arching outward on hillside infestations. The leaves are small, alternate, and lanceolate with irregular serrate margins. Flat-topped clusters have tiny rose-pink flower heads with festooning branch tips and turn into crowded clusters of lustrous brown seed capsules in midsummer. Dense infestations of entangled stems, branches, and foliage exclude other plants and impact animal habitat. Infestations intensify by abundant basal sprouting. Resembles several native and nonnative spiraeas, but is unique in the flat-topped, pink to pink-rose flower clusters and brown fruit clusters, the hairy branchlets and flowers, and lanceolate leaves.

Management strategies:
- Do not plant. Remove prior plantings, and control sprouts and seedlings. Bag and dispose of fruit in a dumpster or burn.
- Treat when new plants are young to prevent seed formation.
- Minimize disturbance within miles of where this plant occurs, and anticipate wider occupation when plants are present before disturbance.
- Do not treat with herbicides when leaves are yellow.
- Manually pull and tree wrench when soil is moist, ensuring removal of the roots.

Recommended control procedures:
- Thoroughly wet all leaves with Garlon 3A or a glyphosate herbicide as a 3-percent solution (12 ounces per 3-gallon mix) in water with a surfactant. Applications may be made almost any time of year, but air temperature must be above 65 °F (18 °C) to ensure absorption by the plant. September is the best time of year for application.
- Cut large stems and immediately treat the stump tops with one of the following herbicides: a glyphosate herbicide or Garlon 3A as a 25-percent solution (3 quarts per 3-gallon mix). ORTHO Brush-B-Gon and Enforcer Brush Killer are effective undiluted for treating cut-stumps and available in retail garden stores (safe to surrounding plants).

Leatherleaf Mahonia

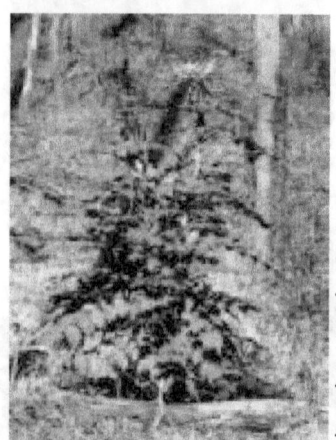

Leatherleaf mahonia or Beale's barberry [*Mahonia bealei* (Fortune) Carrière] is an evergreen shrub, erect and gangly or multistemmed, that grows up to 10 feet (3 m) in height, and branching to 4 to 8 feet (1.2 to 2.4 m) wide from a pronounced root crown (with shallow roots) having yellow centers when cut. Leathery, odd-pinnately compound leaves radiate outward on long stalks with spiny, hollylike leaflets. Terminal, radiating stems of fragrant yellow flowers appear in late winter to spring and yield abundant pale blue fruit in summer that mature to bluish black. Fruits are covered by whitish wax during winter. Species spreads by many bird-dispersed seeds from ornamental plantings and colonizes by basal sprouts. Seed from ripe fruit can immediately germinate. Still widely planted as an ornamental.

Management strategies:

- Do not plant. Remove prior plantings, and control sprouts and seedlings. Bag and dispose of fruit in a dumpster or burn.
- Treat when new plants are young to prevent seed formation.
- Manual pulling is hindered by spiny leaflets.
- Manually pull new seedlings and tree wrench saplings when soil is moist, ensuring removal of all roots.

Recommended control procedures:

- For stems too tall for foliar sprays, cut stems and immediately treat the stump tops with one of the following herbicides: Garlon 4, Garlon 3A, or a glyphosate herbicide as a 25-percent solution (3 quarts per 3-gallon mix). ORTHO Brush-B-Gon and Enforcer Brush Killer are effective undiluted for treating cut-stumps and available in retail garden stores (safe to surrounding plants).
- Thoroughly wet all leaves with one of the following herbicides in water with a surfactant: a glyphosate herbicide or Garlon 3A as a 5-percent solution (20 ounces per 3-gallon mix) during the growing season above 70 °F (21 °C). When nontarget damage is not a concern, use one of the following herbicides: Arsenal AC* as a 0.12-percent solution (0.5 ounce per 3-gallon mix) or Arsenal PowerLine* as a 0.25-percent solution (1 ounce per 3-gallon mix) plus a glyphosate herbicide as a 2-percent solution (8 ounces per 3-gallon mix) plus Escort XP* at 0.4 dry ounce per 3-gallon mix in water. Spray as a low-volume application to lightly wet leaves.

---

* Nontarget plants may be killed or injured by root uptake.

Nonnative Roses

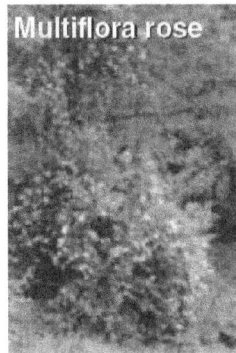  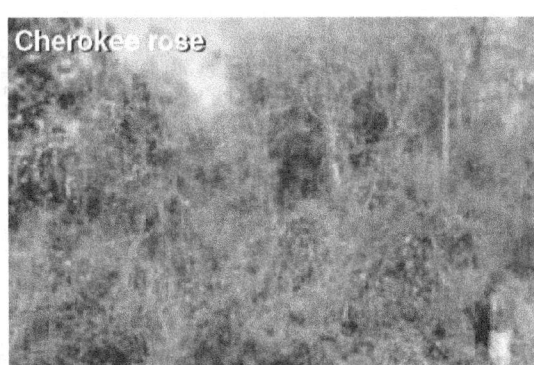 

Multiflora rose (*Rosa multiflora* Thunb.), Macartney rose (*R. bracteata* J.C. Wendl.), Cherokee rose (*R. laevigata* Michx.), and other nonnative roses are all evergreen except multiflora. Roses are all erect, arching, or trailing shrubs to 30 feet (9 m) in height, or long and clump forming. They have pinnately compound leaves with three to nine leaflets and frequent recurved or straight thorns. Clustered or single white-to-pink flowers in early summer yield red rose hips in fall to winter. Roses colonize by prolific sprouting and stems that root when touching the soil and spread by bird- and mammal-dispersed seeds. Resemble native Carolina rose (*R. carolina* L.), swamp rose (*R. palustris* Marsh.), and climbing rose (*R. setigera* Michx.), all of which have pink flowers in spring and nonbristled leafstalk bases, but none form extensive infestations except swamp rose in wet habitat.

Management strategies:
- Do not plant. Remove prior plantings, and control sprouts and seedlings. Bag and dispose of fruit in a dumpster or burn.
- Treat when new plants are young to prevent seed formation.
- Cut and bulldoze when fruit are not present.
- Minimize disturbance within miles of where these plants occur, and anticipate wider occupation if plants are present before disturbance.
- Manual pulling is hindered by thorny branches and is limited to new seedlings.
- Manually pull new seedlings and tree wrench saplings when soil is moist, ensuring removal of all roots.
- Readily eaten by goats and sheep, although this activity also might spread seeds.

Recommended control procedures:
- Thoroughly wet all leaves with one of the following herbicides in water with a surfactant: [April to June (at or near the time of flowering)] Escort XP* at 1 ounce per acre in water (0.2 dry ounce per 3-gallon mix); (August to October) Arsenal AC* as a 1-percent solution (4 ounces per 3-gallon mix) or Escort XP* at 1 ounce per acre in water (0.2 dry ounce per 3-gallon mix); and (May to October) repeated applications of a glyphosate herbicide as a 4-percent solution in water (1 pint per 3-gallon mix), a less-effective treatment that has no soil activity to damage surrounding plants.
- For stems too tall for foliar sprays, apply basal sprays (January to February or May to October) using Garlon 4 as a 20-percent solution (5 pints per 3-gallon mix) in a labeled basal oil product, vegetable oil or mineral oil with a penetrant, or fuel oil or diesel fuel (where permitted); or apply undiluted Pathfinder II. Or cut large stems and immediately treat the stump tops with one of the following herbicides in water with a surfactant: Arsenal AC* as a 10-percent solution (1 quart per 3-gallon mix) or when safety to surrounding vegetation is desired, a glyphosate herbicide as a 20-percent solution (5 pints per 3-gallon mix). ORTHO Brush-B-Gon and Enforcer Brush Killer are effective undiluted for treating cut-stumps and available in retail garden stores (safe to surrounding plants).

---

* Nontarget plants may be killed or injured by root uptake.

Sacred Bamboo, Nandina

Sacred bamboo or nandina (*Nandina domestica* Thunb.) is an evergreen erect shrub to 8 feet (2.5 m) in height, with multiple bushy stems somewhat resembling bamboo and glossy pinnately to bipinnately compound green or reddish leaves. Early summer terminal clusters of tiny white to pinkish flowers yield dangling clusters of red berries in fall and winter. Colonizes by root sprouts and spreads by animal-dispersed seeds.

Management strategies:

- Do not plant. Remove prior plantings, and control sprouts and seedlings. Bag and dispose of fruit in a dumpster or burn.
- Treat when new plants are young to prevent seed formation.
- Manually pull new seedlings and tree wrench saplings when soil is moist, ensuring removal of all roots.
- With ornamental plantings, collect and destroy fruit.

Recommended control procedures:

- Thoroughly wet all leaves with glyphosate herbicide as a 1-percent solution in water (4 ounces per 3-gallon mix) with a surfactant (August to October) or apply a basal spray of Garlon 4 as a 20-percent solution (5 pints per 3-gallon mix) in a labeled basal oil product, vegetable oil or mineral oil with a penetrant, or fuel oil or diesel fuel (where permitted); or apply undiluted Pathfinder II.
- Cut large stems and immediately treat the stump tops with one of the following herbicides in water with a surfactant: Arsenal AC[*] as a 10-percent solution (1 quart per 3-gallon mix) or when safety to surrounding vegetation is desired, a glyphosate herbicide as a 20-percent solution (5 pints per 3-gallon mix). ORTHO Brush-B-Gon and Enforcer Brush Killer are effective undiluted for treating cut-stumps and available in retail garden stores (safe to surrounding plants).

---

[*] Nontarget plants may be killed or injured by root uptake.

Shrubby Nonnative Lespedezas

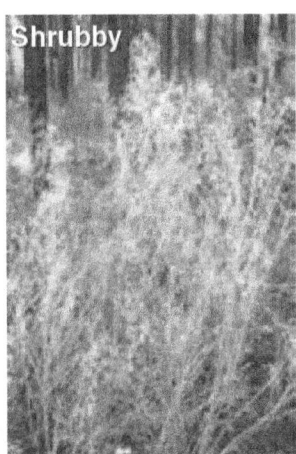

Shrubby lespedeza (*Lespedeza bicolor* Turcz.) and Thunberg's lespedeza [*Lespedeza thunbergii* (DC.) Nakai] are perennial much-branched shrubs 3 to 10 feet (1 to 3 m) in height with stems clustered at the base with Thunberg's and single stems with bicolor, both from woody root crowns. They form dense stands to prevent forest regeneration and land access, and remain standing dormant most of the winter, posing a fire hazard. Many three-leaflet leaves crowd along stems with clusters of small purple-pink pealike flowers that yield single-seeded pods in late summer and remaining in early winter. Seeds are long lived in the soil seed bank and require long-term monitoring after control treatments. When mistakenly planted for wildlife food plots and surface-mine reclamation, they invade adjoining forest edges and open forests.

Management strategies:

- Treat, cut, or mulch when new plants are young to prevent seed formation.
- Manual pulling and weed wrenching is limited to new seedlings when soil is moist to ensure removal of all roots.
- Minimize disturbance within miles of where these plants occur, and anticipate wider occupation if plants are present before disturbance.
- Burning treatments have limited application in most situations and can worsen infestations.
- While grazing by cattle, sheep, and goats can reduce growth, forage quality varies, and grazing also can spread seeds.

Recommended control procedures:

- Thoroughly wet all leaves with one of the following herbicides in water with a surfactant (July to September): Milestone VM* as a 0.1-percent solution (0.5 ounce per 3-gallon mix) applied as 50 gallons per acre, Garlon 4 as a 2-percent solution (8 ounces per 3-gallon mix), or Velpar L* as a 2-percent solution (8 ounces per 3-gallon mix).
- Mowing or mulching 1 to 3 months before herbicide applications can assist control.

---

* Nontarget plants may be killed or injured by root uptake.

Silverthorn, Thorny Olive

Ted Bodner

Silverthorn or thorny olive (*Elaeagnus pungens* Thunb.) is an evergreen, densely bushy shrub 3 to 25 feet (1 to 8 m) in height with long limber projecting shoots that can eventually grow upward spread into tree crowns. Leaves are simple and silver scaly and alternate along shoots with sharp stubby branches, some thorned. Tiny flower clusters appear in fall that yield oblong, red olivelike fruit covered in brown scales in spring. Spreads by animal-dispersed seeds and occurs as scattered individuals, both in the open and under forest shade. Shrubs rapidly increase in size by prolific stem sprouts. Widely planted as an ornamental shrub and infrequently planted for wildlife food.

Management strategies:
- Do not plant. Remove prior plantings, and control sprouts and seedlings. Bag and dispose of fruit in a dumpster.
- Treat when new plants are young to prevent seed formation.
- Cut, mulch, or bulldoze when fruit are not present.
- Minimize disturbance within miles of where this plant occurs, and anticipate wider occupation when plants are present before disturbance.
- Manual pulling and herbicide treatments are hindered by thorny branches.
- Manually pull new seedlings and tree wrench saplings when soil is moist, ensuring removal of all roots and wear eye protection during treatment.
- Burning treatments are suspected of having minimal topkill effect due to absence of litter fuel.
- Readily eaten by goats with potential spread of seed if browsed in spring.

Recommended control procedures:
- Thoroughly wet all leaves with Garlon 3A and Garlon 4 as a 2-percent solution (8 ounces per 3-gallon mix). When nontarget damage is not a concern, use Arsenal AC* or Vanquish* as a 1-percent solution in water (4 ounces per 3-gallon mix) with a surfactant.
- For stems too tall for foliar sprays, apply a basal spray of Garlon 4 as a 20-percent solution (5 pints in a 3-gallon mix) or, where safety to surrounding vegetation is not a concern, Stalker* as a 6- to 9-percent solution (1.5 to 2 pints per 3-gallon mix). Mix either solution in a labeled basal oil product, vegetable oil or mineral oil with a penetrant, or fuel oil or diesel fuel (where permitted) (January to February or May to October).
- Cut large stems and immediately treat the stump tops with one of the following herbicides in water with a surfactant: Arsenal AC* as a 5-percent solution (20 ounces per 3-gallon mix) or when safety to surrounding vegetation is desired, a glyphosate herbicide as a 20-percent solution (5 pints per 3-gallon mix). ORTHO Brush-B-Gon and Enforcer Brush Killer are effective undiluted for treating cut-stumps and available in retail garden stores (safe to surrounding plants).

---

* Nontarget plants may be killed or injured by root uptake.

Tropical Soda Apple

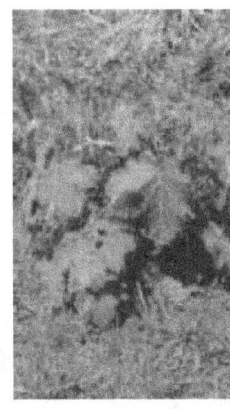

John Everest

Charles Bryson

Tropical soda apple (*Solanum viarum* Dunal) is an upright, thorny perennial subshrub or shrub, 3 to 6 feet (1 to 2 m) in height, characterized by remaining green year-round in most southern locations. It has oak-shaped leaves, clusters of tiny white flowers, and golf-ball sized fruit that are mottled green white turning to yellow in late summer to fall. Immature greenish fruit can contain viable seeds. Fruit have a sweet smell attractive to livestock and wildlife. Spread is now rapid by cattle and other livestock transportation that have consumed the fruit and by wildlife-dispersed seeds as well as seed-contaminated hay, sod, and machinery. Report infestations to county agents for treatment under a federally sponsored eradication program. One leaf feeding biocontrol insect has been released in Florida, Georgia, Alabama, and Texas, and has become established in Florida. Three more biocontrol insects are undergoing further testing and are expected to be released soon. Herbicide treatments should not be applied if heavy defoliation is observed.

Management strategies:
- Do not allow cattle to eat fruit.
- Treat when new plants are young to prevent seed formation.
- Cut and mow when fruit are not present (cutting and mowing is used for stopping fruit production but will not control plants).
- Collect and destroy all fruit.
- Manual pulling is hindered by thorny branches and limited to new seedlings.

Recommended control procedures for isolated sightings:
- Thoroughly wet leaves and stems with one of the following herbicides in water with a surfactant at times of flowering before fruit appear: Garlon 4 (or Remedy® in pastures), Tordon K* ‡, or Arsenal AC* as a 2-percent solution (8 ounces per 3-gallon mix); Milestone VM* as a 0.5-percent solution (2 ounces per 3-gallon mix); Tordon 101* ‡ as a 4-percent solution (1 pint per 3-gallon mix); or a glyphosate herbicide as a 3-percent solution in water (12 ounces per 3-gallon mix).
- If mowing is used to stop fruit production, delay herbicide applications until 50 to 60 days to ensure adequate regrowth.

---

* Nontarget plants may be killed or injured by root uptake.

‡ When using Tordon herbicides, rainfall must occur within 6 days after application for needed soil activation. Tordon herbicides are restricted use pesticides.

Winged Burning Bush

Jane Hargreaves

Winged burning bush or burningbush [*Euonymus alatus* (Thunb.) Siebold] is a deciduous, wing-stemmed, bushy shrub to 12 feet (4 m) in height. Leaves are opposite, obovate, and thin, with both surfaces smooth and hairless. Young stems have four corky wings that run lengthwise. Plants are densely branched with a broad leafy canopy. Leaves are small, obovate and opposite, green in summer and turn bright scarlet-to-purplish red in the fall. Abundant tiny orange fruit appear in late summer as stemmed pairs in leaf axils and turn purple in the fall. Extensively used as an ornamental in the Northeast United States and northern tier of States in the South, with many cultivars. Spreads from plantings and infestations by animal-dispersed seeds, and colonizes by root suckers. Resembles the threatened and endangered native burningbush (*E. atropurpureus* Jacq.), which has erect hairy lower leaf surfaces.

Management strategies:

- Do not plant. Remove prior plantings, and control sprouts and seedlings. Bag and dispose of fruit in a dumpster or burn.
- Treat when new plants are young to prevent seed formation.
- Pull, cut, and treat when fruit are not present.
- Minimize disturbance within miles of where this plant occurs, and anticipate wider occupation when plants are present before disturbance.
- Repeated cutting to groundline commonly recommended for control.
- Manually pull new seedlings and tree wrench saplings when soil is moist, ensuring removal of all roots.

Recommended control procedures:

- Thoroughly wet all leaves with Arsenal AC* or Vanquish* as a 1-percent solution in water (4 ounces per 3-gallon mix) with a surfactant (April to October). When safety to surrounding vegetation is desired, use Garlon 3A or Garlon 4 as a 3-percent solution (12 ounces per 3-gallon mix).
- For stems too tall for foliar sprays, apply Garlon 4 as a 20-percent solution (5 pints per 3-gallon mix) in a labeled basal oil product, vegetable oil, kerosene, or diesel fuel (where permitted) to young bark as a basal spray (January to February or May to October); or undiluted Pathfinder II may be used. Or cut large stems and immediately treat the stump tops with one of the following herbicides in water with a surfactant: Arsenal AC* as a 5-percent solution (20 ounces per 3-gallon mix) or when safety to surrounding vegetation is desired, a glyphosate herbicide as a 20-percent solution (5 pints per 3-gallon mix). ORTHO Brush-B-Gon and Enforcer Brush Killer are effective undiluted for treating cut-stumps and available in retail garden stores (safe to surrounding plants).

---

* Nontarget plants may be killed or injured by root uptake.

Invasive Vines

Invasive vines are some of the most troublesome invaders because they often form the densest infestations, making herbicide applications and other treatments difficult. Many of these vines overtop even mature forests and often form mixed-species infestations with invasive trees and shrubs. Specific herbicides can be effective on certain vines while not controlling but actually releasing any underlying nonnative trees and shrubs. In these situations, select the best herbicide or herbicide mixture for controlling all the invasive species in a mixed-species infestation. Vine control is always difficult because foliar-active herbicides must move through lengthy vines to kill large woody roots and root crowns. Thus, herbicides that have both soil and foliar activity are often the most effective. Only the lower foliage within sprayer reach needs to be treated with a herbicide having both foliar and soil activity. With all herbicides, spray foliage of climbing stems as high as possible and if not controlled, then cut vines. Treat cut stems or allow sprouting before foliar retreatment. When cutting treatments are used, cut as low as possible and also remove the upper portion high enough to prevent regrowth reaching the upper vine to act like a trellis.

Amur Peppervine, Porcelain Berry

    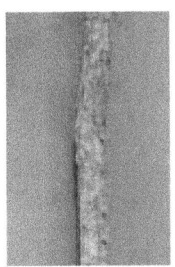

Amur peppervine or porcelain berry [*Ampelopsis brevipedunculata* (Maxim.) Trautv.] is a deciduous, woody vine of the grape family to 20 feet (5 m) long with hairy stems. It runs and climbs over shrub and tree crowns as well as rock faces by clinging forked tendrils, forming thicket and arbor infestations. Heart-shaped leaves can have an entire toothed margin or be symmetrically lobed. Flat clusters of inconspicuous yellowish flowers in spring yield multicolored spherical fruit of white, green, or blue in the fall and winter. Seed spread by animals, water, and gravity. Colonizes by prolific vine growth that roots at nodes when touching the soil. Effective control requires dedicated followup because porcelain berry vines can grow up to 15 feet (4.5 m) in a growing season, especially when rainfall is abundant. Seed may be viable in the soil for several years. Still planted as an ornamental. Resembles the native heartleaf peppervine (*A. cordata* Michx.) with unlobed leaves and hairless stems, which can also form infestations on fences and shrubs.

Management strategies:

- Do not plant. Remove prior plantings, and control sprouts and seedlings. Bag and dispose of fruit in a dumpster or burn.
- Minimize disturbance within miles of where this plant occurs, and anticipate wider occupation when plants are present before disturbance.
- Treat when new plants are young to prevent seed formation.
- Pull, cut, and treat when fruit are not present.
- Manually pull new seedlings when soil is moist, ensuring removal of all roots.

Recommended control procedures:

- Thoroughly wet all leaves with one of the following herbicides in water with a surfactant: a glyphosate herbicide or Garlon 3A as a 2- to 3-percent solution (8 to 12 ounces per 3-gallon mix). When nontarget damage is not a concern, apply Arsenal AC* as a 0.25-percent solution (1 ounce per 3-gallon mix) or Chopper Gen 2* as a 0.5-percent solution (2 ounces per 3-gallon mix) in water.
- To control climbing vines, cut large stems close to ground level and immediately treat the stump tops with Garlon 3A or a glyphosate herbicide with a 25-percent solution (3 quarts per 3-gallon mix). ORTHO Brush-B-Gon and Enforcer Brush Killer are effective undiluted for treating cut-stumps and available in retail garden stores (safe to surrounding plants). For large vines, make stem injections using Arsenal AC*, Garlon 3A, or a glyphosate herbicide with dilutions and cut-spacings specified on the herbicide label (anytime except March and April). The EZ-Ject tree injector assists in reaching through entanglements to treat.

---

* Nontarget plants may be killed or injured by root uptake.

Climbing Yams

  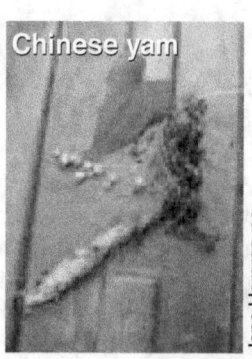  

Air yam (*Dioscorea bulbifera* L.), Chinese yam or cinnamon vine (*D. polystachya* Turczaninow, formerly *D. oppositifolia* L.), and water yam (*D. alata* L.) are herbaceous, high climbing vines to 65 feet (20 m) that cover shrubs and trees in infestations. They have twining and sprawling stems with long-petioled smooth heart-shaped leaves and dangling potato-like tubers (bulbils) that appear at leaf axils and drop to form new plants. Aerial tubers spread downslope and by water and sprout to form new plants. All species also have large tubers underground that make control difficult, but rarely if ever produce seed. Except for south Florida, all vines die back during winter but can cover small trees in a year, with old vines providing trellises for regrowth.

Management strategies:

- Do not plant. Remove prior plantings, and control sprouts and seedlings.
- Bag and dispose of all aerial yams (bulbils) in a dumpster or burn.
- Treat when new plants are young to prevent bulbil formation (rarely if ever produce seed).
- Pull, cut, and treat when fruit are not present.
- Burning and cutting treatments have minimal control due to large underground tubers.

Recommended control procedures:

- Thoroughly wet all leaves with one of the following herbicides in water with a surfactant before aerial bulbils form: Garlon 3A or Garlon 4 as a 2-percent solution (8 ounces per 3-gallon mix). Chinese yam bulbils will take up the herbicide; the other species must be collected and destroyed (not composted).
- For safety to surrounding plants, cut climbing plants just above the soil surface and immediately treat the freshly cut stem with Garlon 3A in a 50-percent solution (6 quarts in a 3-gallon mix).

Five-Leaf Akebia, Chocolate Vine

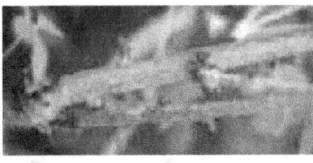

Steven T. Manning

Nancy Loewenstein

Five-leaf akebia or chocolate vine [*Akebia quinata* (Houtt.) Decne.] is a woody, semievergreen or evergreen vine that climbs by twining to dangle and sprawl in tree and shrub crowns to 40 feet (12 m) long. It also can form solid ground cover up to 1 foot (30 cm) deep. Leaves are dark green and palmately compound with five elliptical leaflets on long petioles. Showy, dangling purple flowers infrequently appear with leaves in spring, and some female flowers yield sausage-shaped pods in fall. When the pods are ripe, their skin splits to reveal a pulpy, edible inner core that splits further to expose many (100+) imbedded black seeds. Rarely spreads by animal-dispersed seeds and colonizes by prolific vine growth that root and sprout. Still produced, sold, and planted.

Management strategies:
- Do not plant. Remove prior plantings, and control sprouts and seedlings. Bag and dispose of plants and fruit in a dumpster or burn.
- Treat when new plants are young to prevent seed formation.
- Manually pull new seedlings when soil is moist, ensuring removal of all roots.
- Burning treatments are suspected of having minimal effect due to multiple plants with root crowns that will resprout.

Recommended control procedures:
- Thoroughly wet all leaves with Garlon 3A as a 2- to 3-percent solution (8 to 12 ounces per 3-gallon mix) in water with a surfactant (early to midfall).
- To control climbing vines in trees, cut large stems close to the ground and immediately treat the stump tops with Garlon 3A or a glyphosate herbicide as a 25-percent solution (3 quarts per 3-gallon mix). ORTHO Brush-B-Gon and Enforcer Brush Killer are effective undiluted for treating cut-stumps and available in retail garden stores (safe to surrounding plants). A subsequent foliar application may be required to control new resprouts.

Japanese Honeysuckle

    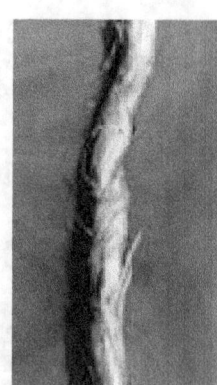

Japanese honeysuckle (*Lonicera japonica* Thunb.) is a semievergreen to evergreen woody vine, high climbing and trailing to 80 feet (24 m), branching and often forming arbors in forest canopies and/or ground cover under canopies. It has opposite leaves, ovate to oblong being green above with the undersurface appearing whitish. Both surfaces smooth to rough hairy. Vines root at nodes when covered by leaves and make control difficult. Often coexists with other invasive plants. Occurs as dense infestations along forest margins and rights-of-way as well as under dense canopies and as arbors high in canopies. Shade tolerant. Persists by large woody rootstocks and spreads mainly by vines rooting at nodes and less by animal-dispersed seeds. Infrequently seeding within forest stands and having very low germination. Seed survival in the soil is less than 2 years. Still planted in wildlife openings and invades surrounding lands. Resembles viney native honeysuckles (*Lonicera* spp.) that usually have reddish hairless stems and hairless leaves and do not form extensive infestations.

Management strategies:

- Do not plant. Remove prior plantings, and control sprouts and seedlings. Bag and dispose of plants and fruit in a dumpster or burn.
- Treat when new plants are young to prevent seed formation.
- Pull, cut, and treat when fruit are not present.
- Manually pull when soil is moist to ensure removal of all stolons and roots.
- Prescribed burning in spring will reduce dense ground mats and sever climbing vines for more effective herbicide treatments to resprouting vines. However, resprouting after one prescribed burn can intensify infestations. Climbing honeysuckle vines can become ladder fuels for fire to reach tree canopies. Repeated burning treatments will not control the plant, and burning is difficult due to absence of fine fuels under honeysuckle mats.
- Readily eaten by goats.

Recommended control procedures:

- When nontarget damage is not a concern, apply Escort XP* with a surfactant to foliage (June to August) either by broadcast spraying 2 ounces per acre in water (0.6 dry ounce per 3-gallon mix) or by spot spraying 2 to 4 ounces per acre in water (0.6 to 1.2 dry ounces per 3-gallon mix).
- Or treat foliage with one of the following herbicides in water with a surfactant (July to October, or during warm days in winter), keeping spray away from desirable plants: a glyphosate herbicide as a 2-percent solution (8 ounces per 3-gallon mix) or Garlon 3A or Garlon 4 as a 3- to 5-percent solution (12 to 20 ounces per 3-gallon mix).
- Or cut large vines just above the soil surface and immediately treat the freshly cut stem with a glyphosate herbicide or Garlon 3A as a 20-percent solution (5 pints per 3-gallon sprayer) in water with a surfactant (July to October). ORTHO Brush-B-Gon and Enforcer Brush Killer are effective for treating cut-stumps and readily available in retail garden stores (safe to surrounding plants) while Brush-B-Gon and Enforcer Brush Killer can be mixed in water and used as foliar sprays.

---

* Nontarget plants may be killed or injured by root uptake.

Kudzu

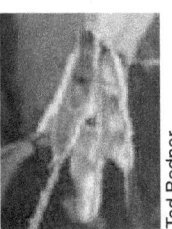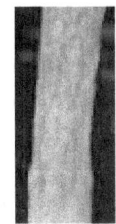

Erwin Chambliss

Ted Bodner

Ted Bodner

Kudzu [*Pueraria montana* (Lour.) Merr.] is a deciduous twining, trailing, mat-forming, woody leguminous vine 35 to 100 feet (10 to 30 m) that forms dense infestations along forest and roadside edges. Leaves have three leaflets with variable lobes. Slender tight clusters of white and violet pealike flowers appear in midsummer to yield clusters of dangling flat pods in fall. Pods fall unopened, and seed are variable in viability across the region. Colonizes by vines rooting at nodes, and spreads by wind-, animal-, and water-dispersed seeds. Large semiwoody tuberous roots with no vine buds reach depths of 3 to 16 feet (1 to 5 m), while the target of control on older plants is a knot- or ball-like root crown on top of the soil surface where vines and roots originate.

Management strategies:

- Do not plant. Remove prior plantings, and control sprouts and seedlings. Bag and dispose of plants and seed pods in a dumpster or burn.
- Treat when new plants are young to prevent spread.
- Anticipate wider occupation when plants are present before disturbance.
- Root crowns can be removed with mattocks, hoes, and saws, while removal of the tuberous taproot is not required for control.
- Mow and then cover for 2 years with plastic sheeting firmly fastened down to gain partial control.
- Repeated multiyear cutting to groundline can achieve control over many years.
- Prescribed burning in spring can clear debris, sever climbing vines, and reveal hazards before summer applications. Repeated burns will not control. Burns are hot especially in winter.
- Tender new shoots are readily eaten by cattle, hogs, and horses, while only goats and sheep will eat semiwoody and woody vines. Prescribed grazing can reduce infestations over several years while pine tree planting in latter years can yield a fully stocked plantation with minimal kudzu.

Recommended control procedures:

- Thoroughly wet all leaves, including those on climbing vines, as high as possible with one of the following herbicides in water with a surfactant: (June to October for successive years when regrowth appears) Tordon 101*‡ as a 3-percent solution (12 ounces per 3-gallon mix) or Tordon K*‡ as a 2-percent solution (8 ounces per 3-gallon mix), either by broadcast or spot spray; (July to early September for successive years) Escort XP* at 3 to 4 ounces per acre (0.8 to 1.2 dry ounces per 3-gallon mix) or Milestone VM* at 7 ounces per acre (2 ounces per 3-gallon mix) in water. When safety to surrounding vegetation is desired, use Transline*† as a 0.5-percent solution in water (2 ounces per 3-gallon mix) or Milestone VM* can safely treat kudzu under many desirable trees and shrubs if herbicide is not applied directly to them.
- For partial control and no soil activity, repeatedly apply Garlon 4 or a glyphosate herbicide as a 4-percent solution in water (1 pint per 3-gallon mix) with a surfactant during the growing season. Or cut large vines and immediately apply the herbicides to the cut surfaces or apply the ready-to-use Pathway* or ORTHO Brush-B-Gon and Enforcer Brush Killer readily available in retail garden stores (safe to surrounding plants). ORTHO Brush-B-Gon, Enforcer Brush Killer, and other "poison ivy" herbicides can be used as foliar sprays.
- To control vines less than 2 inches in diameter, apply basal sprays of Garlon 4 as a 20-percent solution (5 pints per 3-gallon mix) in a labeled basal oil product, vegetable oil, kerosene, or diesel fuel (where permitted) (January to April); or use undiluted Pathfinder II.
- For larger vines, make stem injections using Tordon 101*‡, Stalker*, Arsenal AC*, or a glyphosate herbicide using dilutions and cut-spacings specified on the herbicide label (anytime except March and April).

---

* Nontarget plants may be killed or injured by root uptake.

‡ When using Tordon herbicides, rainfall must occur within 6 days after application for needed soil activation. Tordon herbicides are restricted use pesticides.

† Transline controls a narrow spectrum of plant species.

Nonnative Ivies

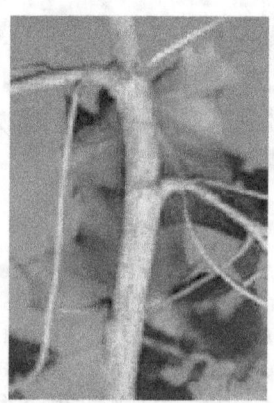

English ivy (*Hedera helix* L.), Atlantic Ivy or Irish ivy [*H. hibernica* (G. Kirchn.) Bean], and colchis or Persian ivy [*H. colchica* (K. Koch)] are evergreen vines that climb to 90 feet (28 m) by clinging roots to encase trees and form dense ground cover. They have thick dark green leaves that are heart shaped with three to five pointed lobes when juvenile and later become lanceolate lacking lobes. Climbing mature plants have terminal flower clusters in summer that yield dark purple berries in winter and spring. Spread by bird-dispersed seeds, and colonize by trailing and climbing vines that root at nodes. English ivy rarely produces fertile seeds along the Gulf Coast. Still widely produced, sold, and planted as ornamentals.

Management strategies:
- Do not plant. Remove prior plantings, and control sprouts and seedlings. Bag and dispose of plants and fruit in a dumpster or burn.
- Treat when new plants are young to prevent seed formation.
- Pull, cut, and treat when fruit are not present (take measures to avoid rashes that can develop from skin contact).
- Repeated cutting and mowing to groundline commonly recommended for control of young infestations.

Recommended control procedures:
- Thoroughly wet all leaves (until runoff) with one of the following herbicides in water with a surfactant (July to October for successive years): Garlon 3A or Garlon 4 as a 3- to 5-percent solution (12 to 20 ounces per 3-gallon mix) or a glyphosate herbicide as a 4-percent solution (1 pint per 3-gallon mix). Use a string trimmer to reduce growth layers and injure leaves for improved herbicide uptake. Cut large vines and apply these herbicides to cut surfaces.
- Or apply basal sprays of Garlon 4 as a 20-percent solution in a labeled basal oil product, vegetable oil, kerosene, or diesel fuel (where permitted) (5 pints per 3-gallon mix); or apply undiluted Pathfinder II to large vines, avoiding the bark of desirable trees.

Nonnative Wisterias

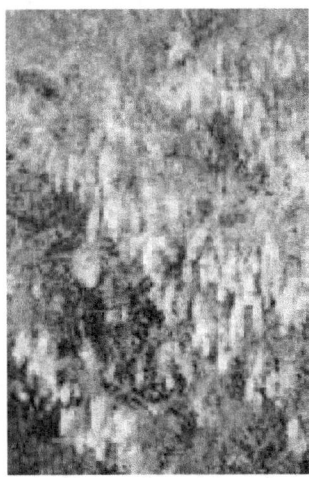

Chinese wisteria [*Wisteria sinensis* (Sims) DC.] and Japanese wisteria [*W. floribunda* (Willd.) DC.] are deciduous high climbing, twining, or trailing leguminous woody vines with long pinnately compound leaves and showy dangling clusters of spring flowers that appear before leaves. Chinese and Japanese wisterias are difficult to distinguish due to hybridization. Both colonize by vines twining and covering shrubs and trees and by runners that root at nodes when vines are covered by leaflitter. Seeds are water dispersed along riparian areas, but the large size of the seeds is a deterrent to animal dispersal. Still sold and planted with many cultivars. Resemble native or naturalized American wisteria [*W. frutescens* (L.) Poir.], which occurs in wet forests and edges and sometimes forms large entanglements but flowers in June to August after leaves develop.

Management strategies:

- Do not plant. Remove prior plantings, and control sprouts and seedlings. Bag and dispose of plants and fruit in a dumpster or burn.
- Treat when new plants are young to prevent seed formation.
- Pull, cut, and treat when pods are not present.
- Anticipate wider occupation when plants are present before disturbance.
- Manually pull new seedlings when soil is moist, ensuring removal of all roots.
- Prescribed burning in spring can clear debris, sever climbing vines, and reveal hazards before summer applications. Repeated burning will not control.

Recommended control procedures:

- Thoroughly wet all leaves (until runoff) with one of the following herbicides in water with a surfactant: (July to October for successive years when regrowth appears) Tordon 101[*][‡] as a 3-percent solution (12 ounces per 3-gallon mix) or Tordon K[*][‡] as a 2-percent solution (8 ounces per 3-gallon mix), or when soil activity is not desired: Garlon 4 as a 4-percent solution (1 pint per 3-gallon mix); (July to September for successive years when regrowth appears); Transline[*][†] as a 0.5-percent solution in water (2 ounces per 3-gallon mix); or (September to October with repeated applications) a glyphosate herbicide as a 4-percent solution (1 pint per 3-gallon mix).
- For large vines, make stem injections using Arsenal AC[*], Garlon 3A, or a glyphosate herbicide using dilutions and cut-spacings specified on the herbicide label (anytime except March and April). The EZ-Ject tree injector assists in reaching through entanglements to treat. Spray the length of large surface vines using Garlon 4 as a 20-percent solution in a labeled basal oil product, vegetable oil, kerosene, or diesel fuel (where permitted) (5 pints per 3-gallon mix); or apply undiluted Pathfinder II to large vines, avoiding the bark of desirable trees.

---

[*] Nontarget plants may be killed or injured by root uptake.

[‡] When using Tordon herbicides, rainfall must occur within 6 days after application for needed soil activation. Tordon herbicides are restricted use pesticides.

[†] Transline controls a narrow spectrum of plant species.

82

Oriental Bittersweet

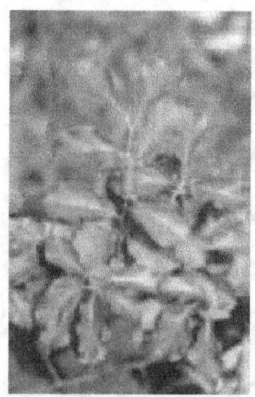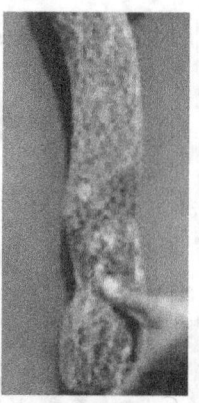

Jane Hargreave

Oriental bittersweet (*Celastrus orbiculatus* Thunb.) is an attractive but very invasive deciduous, twining, and climbing woody vine to 60 feet (20 m) with drooping branches in tree crowns, forming thicket and arbor infestations. It has alternate elliptic-to-rounded leaves 1.2- to 5-inches (3 to 12 cm) long. Female plants have axillary dangling clusters of inconspicuous yellowish flowers that yield spherical fruit capsules, green maturing to yellow, that split to reveal three-parted showy scarlet fleshy-covered seeds, which remain through winter at most leaf axils. Colonizes by prolific vine growth that root at nodes and seedlings from prolific seed spread mainly by birds, possibly other animals and humans collecting and discarding decorative fruit-bearing vines. Seeds are highly viable, germinate even under dense shade, and after germination, grow rapidly when exposed to light. Most seed will germinate but only remain viable for 1 year in the soil. Resembles American bittersweet (*C. scandens* L.), which has only terminal white flower clusters that yield orange fruit capsules; leaves usually twice as large but absent among the flowers and fruit. Hybridization occurs between the two species.

Management strategies:

- Do not plant. Remove prior plantings, and control sprouts and seedlings. Bag and dispose of plants and fruit in a dumpster or burn.
- Treat when new plants are young to prevent seed formation.
- Pull, cut, and treat when fruit are not present.
- Minimize disturbance within miles of where this plant occurs, and anticipate wider occupation when plants are present before disturbance.
- Repeated cutting to groundline commonly recommended for control, while root sprouts might worsen some infestations.
- Manually pull new seedlings and tree wrench large vines when soil is moist, ensuring removal of all roots. Outlying large vines that remain after treatments will resprout, even under a forest canopy.
- Burning treatments are suspected of having minimal topkill effect due to scant litter.
- Readily eaten by goats while seed spread is possible.

Recommended control procedures:

- Thoroughly wet all leaves with one of the following herbicides in water with a surfactant (July to October): Garlon 4, Garlon 3A, or a glyphosate herbicide as a 3-percent solution (12 ounces per 3-gallon mix).
- For stems too tall for foliar sprays, to control vines less than 1-inch diameter, apply Garlon 4 as a 20-percent solution (5 pints per 3-gallon mix) in a labeled basal oil product, vegetable oil, kerosene, or diesel fuel (where permitted); or apply undiluted Pathfinder II as a basal spray to the lower 2 feet of stems. Or cut large stems and immediately treat the cut surfaces with one of the following herbicides in water with a surfactant: Garlon 4 or a glyphosate herbicide as a 25-percent solution (32 ounces per 1-gallon mix). ORTHO Brush-B-Gon and Enforcer Brush Killer are effective for treating cut-stumps and readily available in retail garden stores (safe to surrounding plants). Winter applications are effective.
- For large vines, make stem injections using Arsenal AC[*], Garlon 3A, or a glyphosate herbicide using dilutions and cut-spacings specified on the herbicide label (anytime except March and April). The EZ-Ject tree injector assists in reaching through entanglements to treat, and the glyphosate shells have been found effective in winter.

---

[*] Nontarget plants may be killed or injured by root uptake.

Vincas, Periwinkles

Bigleaf periwinkle

Common periwinkle

Bigleaf periwinkle

Bigleaf periwinkle

Nancy Loewenstein

Common periwinkle (*Vinca minor* L.) and bigleaf periwinkle (*V. major* L.) are evergreen (leaves always present), somewhat woody, trailing or scrambling vines to 3 feet (1 m) long and upright to 1 foot (30 cm) that form dense ground cover. They have opposite lanceolate-to-heart-shaped leaves and five-petaled pinwheel-shaped violet single flowers. They form mats and extensive infestations even under forest canopies by vines rooting at nodes. Viable seed appear to be produced only rarely.

Management strategies:

- Do not plant. Remove prior plantings, and control sprouts and seedlings. Bag and dispose of plants in a dumpster or burn.
- Treat when new plants are young.
- Mowing treatments or injury of the leaves by a string trimmer immediately prior to herbicide spraying improves control with herbicides lacking soil activity.
- Burning treatments are suspected of having minimal effect.

Recommended control procedures:

- Thoroughly wet all leaves (until runoff) with one of the following herbicides in water with a surfactant (July to October for successive years): Tordon 101[*][‡] as a 3-percent solution (12 ounces per 3-gallon mix) or Tordon K[*][‡] as a 2-percent solution (8 ounces per 3-gallon mix); or in spring when safety to surrounding vegetation is desired before stands become dense with new growth, Garlon 4 as a 4-percent solution (1 pint per 3-gallon mix); or during the growing season, repeatedly apply Garlon 4 or a glyphosate herbicide as a 2-percent solution in water (8 ounces per 3-gallon mix) with a surfactant. In winter, herbicide treatments should be limited to warm days.

[*] Nontarget plants may be killed or injured by root uptake.

[‡] When using Tordon herbicides, rainfall must occur within 6 days after application for needed soil activation. Tordon herbicides are restricted use pesticides.

Winter Creeper

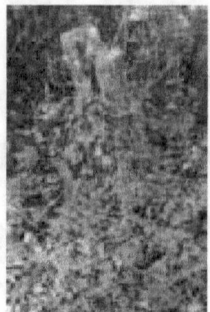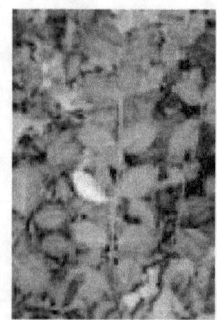

Winter creeper or climbing euonymus [*Euonymus fortunei* (Turcz.) Hand.-Maz.] is an evergreen shrub to 3 feet (1 m) in height and woody trailing vine to 40 to 70 feet (12 to 22 m) that forms a dense ground cover and climbs trees and rocks by clinging aerial roots along stems. It has leaves that are opposite, thick, and dark green or green-white variegated on green stems. Pinkish-to-red capsules split open in fall to expose orange fleshy-covered seeds. Species colonizes by trailing and climbing vines that root at nodes, and fleshy-coated seeds are spread by birds, other animals, and water. Still produced, sold, and planted as an ornamental with several cultivars.

Management strategies:

- Do not plant. Remove prior plantings, and control sprouts and seedlings. Bag and dispose of plants and fruit in a dumpster or burn.
- Treat when new plants are young to prevent seed formation.
- Pull, cut, and treat when fruit are not present.
- Repeated cutting to groundline commonly recommended for control.
- Injury of the leaves by a string trimmer immediately prior to herbicide spraying can improve control with those lacking soil activity.
- Cut all vertical climbing stems to prevent fruiting and spread of seed by birds.
- Burning treatments are suspected of having minimal effect.

Recommended control procedures:

- When nontarget damage is not a concern, thoroughly wet all leaves (until runoff) with one of the following herbicides in water with a surfactant (July to October for successive years): Tordon 101[*][‡] as a 3-percent solution (12 ounces per 3-gallon mix) or Tordon K[*][‡] as a 2-percent solution (8 ounces per 3-gallon mix).
- When safety to surrounding vegetation is desired, apply Garlon 4 or a glyphosate herbicide as a 4-percent solution (1 pint per 3-gallon mix) in water with a surfactant, preferably in the fall a month before expected frost, and repeat in the spring to regrowth.
- For large vines, make stem injections using Arsenal AC[*], Garlon 3A, or a glyphosate herbicide using dilutions and cut-spacings specified on the herbicide label (anytime except March and April).

---

[*] Nontarget plants may be killed or injured by root uptake.

[‡] When using Tordon herbicides, rainfall must occur within 6 days after application for needed soil activation. Tordon herbicides are restricted use pesticides.

Invasive Grasses and Canes

Nonnative grasses and bamboos continue to spread along highway rights-of-way and, thus, gain access to adjoining lands. Most nonnative invasive grasses are highly flammable; increase fire intensities, subjecting firefighters to higher risk; and spread rapidly after wildfire or prescribed burns. Invasive grasses have become one of the most insidious problems in the field of wildlife management on pasture and prairie lands because they have low wildlife value and leave little room for native plants. Repeated applications of herbicides are required for control with establishment of native plants. Long established bamboo infestation continue to expand without control treatments.

Bamboos

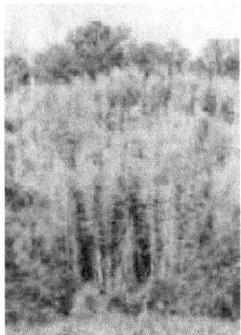    

Golden bamboo (*Phyllostachys aurea* Carrière ex A. Rivière & C. Rivière) and other nonnative bamboos (*Phyllostachys* spp. and *Bambusa* spp.) are perennial infestation-forming canes 16 to 40 feet (5 to 12 m) in height. They have jointed cane stems and bushy tops of lanceolate leaves in fan clusters on jutting branches, often golden green. Plants arise from large branched rhizomes, and infestations rapidly expand after disturbance. Seeds rarely, if ever, produced—potentially once every 50 to 100 years. Still sold and planted as ornamentals. Bamboos are very difficult to eradicate. Resemble switch-cane [*Arundinaria gigantea* (Walter) Muhl. and other *Arundinara* spp.], the only native bamboolike canes in the South, distinguished by a lower height—usually only 6 to 8 feet (2 to 2.5 m)—and persistent sheaths on the stem and absence of long opposite horizontal branches. Also resemble the invasive giant reed (*Arundo donax* L.) described in this book.

Management strategies:
- Do not plant. Remove prior plantings.
- Bulldoze and root rake to excavate root crowns and rhizomes, pile, and burn. Caution: Do not bulldoze bamboo infestations where blackbird species frequently roost because the infectious fungus, **histoplasmosis** can be present in the soil and cause deadly lung infections.
- Repeated cutting to groundline will not yield control but can assist herbicide applications to resprouts.
- Burning treatments are suspected of having minimal topkill effect due to scant litter.

Recommended control procedures:
- Cut large stems and apply foliar sprays to resprout tips when plants are 3 to 4 feet tall, or use restricted spray nozzles and increased spray pressures to treat leaves as high as possible. When damage of nontarget plants is a concern, repeatedly apply a glyphosate herbicide as a 10-percent solution (1 quart per 3-gallon mix) in water with a surfactant. When there are no concerns of nontarget plant damage, thoroughly wet all leaves and sprouts with Arsenal AC[*] as a 1-percent solution (4 ounces per 3-gallon mix) in water with a surfactant. For greatest effectiveness, use a combination of the two herbicides. Treat in September or October with multiple applications to regrowth when adequate foliage is present.
- Cut just above ground level between stem sections and immediately apply into the stem cup a double-strength batch of the same herbicide or herbicide mixture in September or October.
- For treatment of extensive infestations in forest situations, apply Velpar L[*] to the soil surface as spots in a grid pattern at spacings specified on the herbicide label at 2 gallons of herbicide per acre.

[*] Nontarget plants may be killed or injured by root uptake.

Chinese Silvergrass

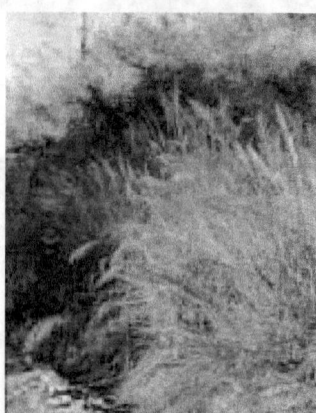   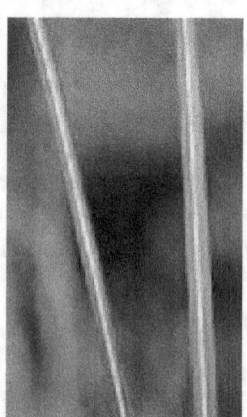

Chinese silvergrass (*Miscanthus sinensis* Andersson) is a tall, densely tufted, perennial grass, 5 to 10 feet (1.5 to 3 m) in height from a perennial root crown. It has long, slender, and upright-to-arching leaves with whitish upper midveins and many loosely plumed panicles turning silvery to pinkish in fall. Dried grass remains standing with some seed heads during winter, but seed viability is variable depending on cultivar and location. Spreading invasive cultivars have viable seeds. Species forms extensive infestations by escaping from older ornamental plantings to roadsides, forest margins, rights-of-way, and adjacent disturbed sites, especially after burning. Presently only an invasive problem in the northern tier of States in the southern region, while projected widespread plantings for biomass and biofuels could result in aggravated problems.

Management strategies:

- Do not plant. Remove prior plantings, and control sprouts and seedlings. Bag and dispose of plants and seed heads in a dumpster or burn.
- Treat when new plants are young to prevent seed formation.
- Minimize disturbance within miles of where fertile plants occur, and anticipate wider occupation if plants are present or adjacent before disturbance.
- Do not mow when there are seed heads.
- Burning treatments are suspected of having minimal effect, and dormant standing infestations in winter are highly flammable and pose a fire hazard.

Recommended control procedures:

- Thoroughly wet all leaves with one of the following herbicides in water with a surfactant (September or October with multiple applications to regrowth): Arsenal AC[*] as a 1-percent solution (4 ounces per 3-gallon mix). When safety to surrounding vegetation is desired, a glyphosate herbicide as a 4-percent solution (1 pint per 3-gallon mix) only to the target plants; or a combination of the two herbicides, Arsenal AC[*] as a 0.5-percent solution (2 ounces per 3-gallon mix) plus a glyphosate herbicide as a 4-percent solution (2 ounces plus 1 pint per 3-gallon mix). Repeat applications when new growth reaches 2 feet (60 cm) in height.

---

[*] Nontarget plants may be killed or injured by root uptake.

Cogongrass

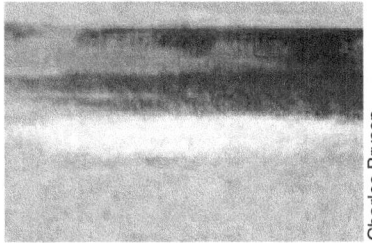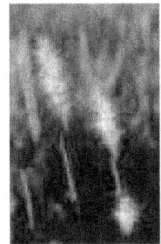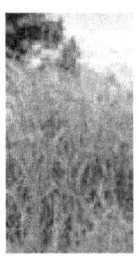

Charles Bryson

Cogongrass [*Imperata cylindrica* (L.) P. Beauv.] and the closely related native, Brazilian satintail (*I. brasiliensis* Trin.), are aggressive, colony-forming dense erect perennial grasses 1 to 6 feet (30 to 180 cm) in height. Hybridization is probable and makes differentiation difficult. Both have tufts of long leaves hiding short stems, yellow-green blades (each with an offcenter midvein and finely saw-toothed margins), and silver-plumed flowers and seeds in spring (sporadically year-round). Seed are dispersed by wind and on contaminated clothing, equipment, and products like pinestraw mulch and fill materials. Seed viability appears at this time to be significantly less in northern Florida and southern Georgia and higher in southern Alabama and Mississippi.

Dense stands of dried plants remain standing during winter to present a severe fire hazard, while remaining green year-round in central and southern Florida. These species burn hot even when green.

Infestations form dense rhizome mats making eradication difficult, because abundant shoot and rhizome buds usually sprout after treatment or lay dormant to sprout within months. Rhizomes are sharp tipped and can pierce roots of other plants. Older infestations will be more difficult to control than new invasions that occur as circular patches.

Both species are Federal and State noxious weeds, while red-tipped cultivars are still sold and planted in many Southern States. These cultivars, bred for cold hardiness, have viable pollen that might spread to the invasive cogongrass plants. Red cultivars can revert to the green aggressive type. Some Southern States prohibit the sale of the red cultivars. Visit www.cogongrass.org and other State cogongrass Web sites for more details. Resemble Johnsongrass [*Sorghum halepense* (L.) Pers.]; purpletop [*Tridens flavus* (L.) Hitchc.]; silver plumegrass [*Saccharum alopecuroidum* (L.) Nutt.]; and sugarcane plumegrass [*S. giganteum* (Walter) Pers.]—all having a stem, do not produce fluffy seed heads, and no sharp-tipped rhizomes jutting up from the soil surface. Also resemble longleaf woodoats [*Chasmanthium sessiliflorum* (Poir.) Yates] that occurs in shaded colonies in forests but lacks offcenter midveins and silky flowers having tufts of spiked flowers and seeds along a slender stalk.

Management strategies:
- Do not plant the red-tipped cultivars (Japanese bloodgrass and Red Baron). Remove prior plantings, and control sprouts and seedlings.
- Treat when new plants are young and located through frequent surveillance of lands in infested zones.
- Minimize disturbance within miles of where this plant occurs, and anticipate wider occupation when plants are present or adjacent before disturbance.
- Repeated cultivation and planting of aggressive grasses or herbicide resistant crops can restore pastures and croplands.
- Burning and bush-mowing treatments can remove standing plants for more efficient herbicide treatments. However, burning usually causes rapid infestation expansion and can kill native shrubs and trees that constrain spread.
- Do not use or transport fill dirt, rock, hay, or pinestraw from infested lands.
- Seed production can be stopped by mowing, burning, or herbicide treatments in early stages of flowering or even shortly before flowering. However, these treatments can prompt later flowering/seeding as well.
- Clean seed and rhizomes from equipment and personnel working in infestations before leaving the infested site.
- Forage quality is low, eaten only when shoots are young and tender by horses, goats, sheep, mules, and some cattle.

Recommended control procedures:
- Thoroughly wet all leaves with one of the following herbicides in water with a surfactant when grass is actively growing and at least 1to 2 feet high or older growth from June to September: Chopper Gen2[*] as a 2-percent solution (8 ounces per 3-gallon mix) or Arsenal AC[*] as a 1-percent solution (4 ounces per 3-gallon mix). Repeat applications in subsequent years may be required for eradication. A glyphosate herbicide may be tank mixed as a 2- to 5-percent solution with Chopper Gen2[*] at 2 percent (8 ounces per 3-gallon mix) or Arsenal AC[*] at 1 percent (4 ounces per 3-gallon mix). This treatment will accelerate burndown of actively growing shoots but may not improve rhizome kill.
- When safety to surrounding vegetation is desired (especially hardwoods, shrubs, and pines), apply a glyphosate herbicide as a 2- to 5-percent solution (8 to 20 ounces per 3-gallon mix). Two applications per growing season (just before flowering in spring and again in late summer to regrowth) are typically necessary. Apply in successive years when regrowth is present until no live rhizomes are observed for eradication; at the same time promote or establish desirable plants.

[*] Nontarget plants may be killed or injured by root uptake.

Giant Reed

Giant reed (*Arundo donax* L.) is a cane that grows up to 20 feet (6 m) in height from spreading tuberous rhizomes and forms thickets in distinct clumps. It has cornlike gray-green and hairless leaves jutting alternately from stems and drooping at the ends. Erect plumelike terminal panicles of flowers and seed heads appear in late summer and persist through winter. Seed are not viable. Dried plants remain standing in winter and spring while low and sheltered plants may remain green. Species spreads by movement of stem and rhizome parts in soil or by road-shoulder mowing and grading and by running water. Each stem and rhizome section has a viable bud. Only an invasive problem in local infestations, while projected widespread plantings for biomass and biofuels could result in severe problems. Closely resembles common reed [*Phragmites australis* (Cav.) Trin. ex Steud.], which has similar large hairy seed heads, but not erect and fanned in a loose plume and which occurs mainly near swamps, marshes, and wet habitats in extensive infestations.

Management strategies:

- Oppose widespread planting of this species for fiber or fuels.
- Do not plant. Remove prior plantings, and control sprouts. Bag and dispose of plants in a dumpster or burn.
- Frequent repeated cutting to groundline may result in control.
- Burning treatments are suspected of having minimal effect due to underground rhizomes.

Recommended control procedures:

- Thoroughly wet all leaves with one of the following herbicides in water with a surfactant (September or October with multiple applications to regrowth): when safety to surrounding plants is desired, a glyphosate herbicide as a 4-percent solution (1 pint per 3-gallon mix) directed at this plant and away from surrounding plants; Arsenal AC* as a 1-percent solution (4 ounces per 3-gallon mix); or a combination of the two herbicides; Arsenal AC* as a 0.5-percent solution (2 ounces per 3-gallon mix) and a glyphosate herbicide as a 4-percent solution (1 pint per 3-gallon mix).

* Nontarget plants may be killed or injured by root uptake.

Johnsongrass

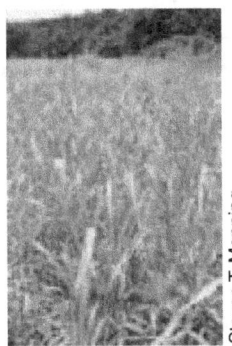 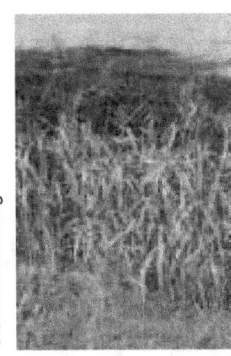    

Steven T. Manning • Ted Bodner • Ted Bodner • Ted Bodner • Ted Bodner

Johnsongrass [*Sorghum halepense* (L.) Pers.] is an erect, perennial, warm-season grass, with stout round stemmed, 3 to 8 feet (1 to 2.5 m) tall, branching from the base. It has long and wide green leaves with prominent white midveins and tall cone-shaped reddish flower heads in midsummer that yield abundant husked tiny blackish seeds in fall. Persists and colonizes by rhizomes and spreads by seeds. New plants can produce seeds the first year. Each rhizome segment can sprout. Occurs as dense colonies in old fields, along field margins, and rights-of-way where it invades new forest plantations, open forests, and forest openings. Rapidly spreading along roadsides through mowing. Still planted as a pasture grass in some subregions, even though the plant can be toxic to grazing animals after frost or if it is fertilized or drought stricken. Resembles several stout grasses when young, while the seed head shape is more unique to the other sorghum species that are crops and the common native grass purpletop tridens [*Tridens flavus* (L.) Hitchc.] whose leaves have only a thin whitish midvein, the leaf base is often reddish tinged, and seeds are maroon on distinctly drooping seed head branches.

Management strategies:

- Do not plant.
- Treat when new plants are young to prevent seed formation.
- Pull and excavate all rhizomes, cut, and treat before seed are present.
- Minimize disturbance within miles of where this plant occurs, and anticipate wider occupation when plants are present before disturbance.
- Burning treatments are suspected of having effect due to persistent rhizomes.
- Sparingly eaten by cattle, sheep, and goats, while toxic at times, especially to horses.

Recommended control procedures:

- Thoroughly wet all leaves with one of the following herbicides in water with a surfactant (June to October with multiple applications applied to regrowth).
  - Recommendation for mature grass control: apply Outrider[*] as a broadcast spray at 0.75 to 2 ounces per acre (0.2 to 0.6 dry ounce per 3-gallon mix) plus a nonionic surfactant to actively growing Johnsongrass. For handheld and high-volume sprayers, apply 1 ounce of Outrider[*] per 100 gallons of water plus a nonionic surfactant at 0.25 percent. Outrider[*] is a selective herbicide that can be applied over the top of other grasses to kill Johnsongrass, or apply Plateau[*] as a 0.25-percent solution (1 ounce per 3-gallon mix) when plants are 18 to 24 inches (45 to 60 cm) tall or larger.
  - Recommendation for seedling control: apply Journey[*] as a 0.3-percent solution (1.2 ounces per 3-gallon mix) before Johnsongrass sprouts and when desirable species are dormant or apply a glyphosate herbicide as a 2-percent solution (8 ounces per 3-gallon mix) directed at the infestation.

---

[*] Nontarget plants may be killed or injured by root uptake.

Nepalese Browntop, Japanese Stiltgrass

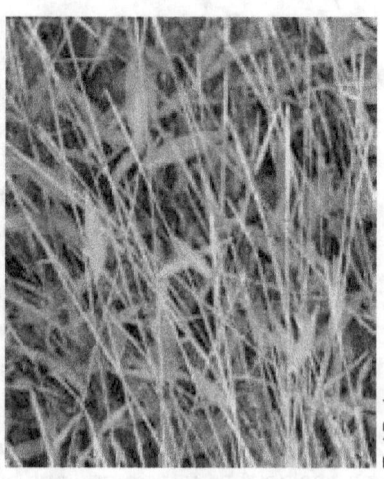

Nepalese browntop or Japanese stiltgrass [*Microstegium vimineum* (Trin.) A. Camus] is a sprawling, dense, mat-forming annual grass, 0.5 to 3 feet (15 to 90 cm) long with stems growing to 1 to 3 feet (30 to 89 cm) in height, often bending over and rooting at nodes to form extensive infestations. It has alternate, lanceolate leaf blades to 4 inches (10 cm) long with offcenter veins and thin seed heads in summer and fall. Dried whitish-tan grass remains standing or matted in winter. One of the region's most severe invasive plants, it flourishes on alluvial floodplains and streamsides, mostly colonizing flood-scoured banks, due to water dispersal of seed and flood tolerance. It is also common in forest edges, roadsides, and trailsides, as well as damp fields, swamps, lawns, and ditches. It occurs up to 4,000 feet (1200 m) elevation and is very shade tolerant. Consolidates occupation by prolific seeding, with each plant producing 100 to 1,000 seeds that can remain viable in the soil for up to 3 years. Hidden seeds within leaf sheaves are produced in early summer. Spreads on trails and recreational areas by seeds hitchhiking on hikers' and visitors' shoes and clothes.

Management strategies:

- Apply herbicide and mowing treatments to stop seed production.
- Hand pulling alone or hand pulling followed by a summer herbicide application result in the most plant diversity compared to broadcast glyphosate treatments, while control and diversity will only be maintained with repeated hand pulling.
- Treat when new plants are young to prevent seed formation, and be aware that early summer self-pollinated seeds are hidden inside the leaf sheaves.
- Clean shoes, clothes, dogs, and equipment of tiny seeds before leaving infested areas.
- Minimize disturbance within miles of where this plant occurs, and anticipate wider occupation when plants are present before disturbance.
- Infestations result in a widespread and dense layer of fine fuels in winter that can result in intense fires causing damage to native plants. Prescribed burning can promote spread of existing infestations..

Recommended control procedures:

- Apply a glyphosate herbicide as a 0.5- to 2-percent solution in water (2 to 8 ounces per 3-gallon mix) with a surfactant in early summer; or apply Fusilade® DX or Plateau* (see label) in summer for situations that require more selective control and less impact on associated plants (hand weeding a month prior to these treatments will increase control and revegetation diversity).
- Repeat treatments for several years to control abundant germinating seeds. Mowing or pulling just before seed set will also prevent seed buildup in the soil seed bank. An early summer seed crop is hidden inside the leaf sheaves.

---

* Nontarget plants may be killed or injured by root uptake.

Tall Fescue

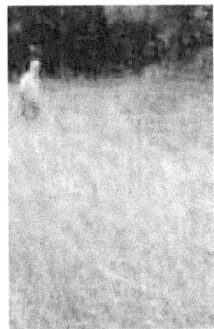   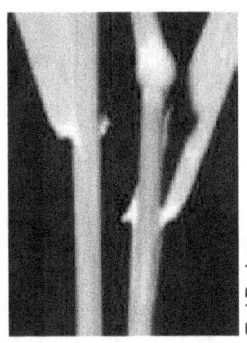

Tall fescue [*Schedonorus phoenix* (Scop.) Holub] [formerly *S. arundinaceus* (Schreb.) Dumort., *Lolium arundinaceum* (Schreb.) S.J. Darbyshire, *Festuca arundinacea* Schreb., *and F. elatior* L. ssp. *arundinacea* (Schreb.) Hack.] is an erect, tufted cool-season perennial grass, 2 to 4 feet (60 to 120 cm) in height. It has whitish-eared areas where leaf blades connect to the stem, and the stem has swollen nodes. Dark-green seedstalks and leaves appear in late winter, usually flowering in spring (infrequently in late summer). This grass is dormant in midsummer. Most tall fescue is infected with a fungus that can reduce weight gains and lower reproductive rates in livestock, while adversely affecting the nutrition of songbirds and the Canada goose (*Branta canadensis*). Tall fescue monocultures are generally poor habitat for wildlife, especially ground nesting birds. Still sold and widely planted for soil stabilization, pastures, and reclamation, with many cultivars available. Species spreads by expanding root crowns and somewhat less by seeds.

Management strategies:

- Do not plant. Remove prior plantings, and control sprouts and seedlings. Bag and dispose of plants and seeds in a dumpster or burn.
- Treat when new plants are young to prevent seed formation.
- Pull, cut, and treat when seed are not present.
- Minimize disturbance where this plant occurs, and anticipate wider occupation when plants are present before disturbance.
- Early spring burning, if repeated, inhibits fescue and encourages native warm-season grasses.
- Readily eaten by most livestock although toxic in certain seasons.

Recommended control procedures:

- On forest lands, apply a glyphosate herbicide as a 5-percent solution in water (2 quarts per 10 gallons mix per acre) or when there are no concerns for surrounding plants, Arsenal AC[*] as a 1-percent solution (25 ounces per 20 gallons mix per acre) in spring.
- On noncroplands, apply 10 to 12 ounces of Plateau[*] or 20 to 24 ounces of Journey[*] per 20 gallons mix per acre (consult the label for additives) in spring. Mixing Plateau with a glyphosate herbicide will improve control but may damage associated native plants. Vantage (sethoxydim), Poast® (sethoxydim), Assure® II (quizalofop), and Select® 2 EC (clethodim) may be useful in certain situations for establishing or releasing native grasses, but they are usually more costly than using Journey or a glyphosate mix with Plateau.

---

[*] Nontarget plants may be killed or injured by root uptake.

Weeping Lovegrass

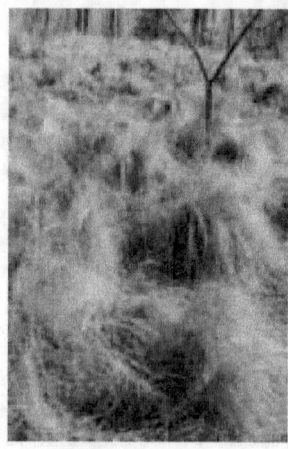

Weeping lovegrass [*Eragrostis curvula* (Schrad.) Nees] is a densely clumping perennial, warm-season grass, formed from flattened basally interconnected plants of long, thin, and wiry basal leaves that arch and droop in all directions and eventually touch the ground (thus, the common name "weeping"). Tall laterally branched flower stalks appear in early summer to 6 feet (2 m) and persist with seed during the early winter having varying viability. Tolerant to fire and drought, and bred for cold tolerance. Clumps increase by tillering new plants at the base, and seedlings intensify infestations. Seed dispersed by water, contaminated equipment and soil, and planting. Occurs as dense colonies in old fields, along field margins, and rights-of-way where it invades new forest plantations, open forests, forest openings, and special habitats like native prairies. Poor habitat for wildlife, especially ground nesting and foraging birds.

Management strategies:

- Do not plant. Remove prior plantings, and control sprouts and seedlings. Bag and dispose of plants and seed in a dumpster or burn.
- Treat when new plants are young to prevent seed formation.
- Minimize disturbance within miles of where this plant occurs, and anticipate wider occupation when plants are present before disturbance.
- Pull, cut, and treat when seed are not present.
- Burning treatments are suspected of having minimal topkill effect due to scant litter.
- Sparingly eaten by most livestock with varying nutritional value.

Recommended control procedures:

- Thoroughly wet all leaves with one of the following herbicides in water with a surfactant: a glyphosate herbicide as a 2-percent solution (8 ounces per 3-gallon mix), Arsenal AC* as a 0.5 percent solution (2 ounces per 3-gallon mix), or Arsenal PowerLine* as a 0.75-percent solution (3 ounces per 3-gallon mix). All applications should be made in early summer when foliage is developed and seeds have not been produced.

---

* Nontarget plants may be killed or injured by root uptake.

Invasive Ferns

Japanese climbing fern [*Lygodium japonicum* (Thunb.) Sw.] is presently the only widespread nonnative invasive fern in the temperate parts of the South. Old world or small-leaf climbing fern [*L. microphyllum* (Cav.) R. Br.] is a severe invasive in south to central Florida.

Japanese Climbing Fern

   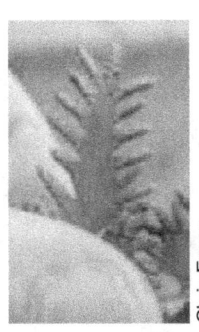 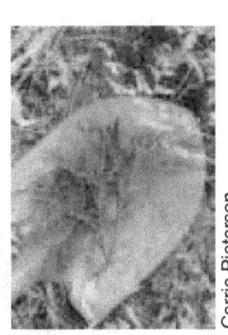

Chris Evans

Corrie Pieterson

Japanese climbing fern [*Lygodium japonicum* (Thunb.) Sw.] is a climbing and twining, perennial viney fern to 90 feet (30 m), often forming mats of shrub- and tree-covering infestations. It has lacy finely divided leaves along green-to-orange-to-black wiry vines. Tan-brown fronds persist in winter, while others remain green in Florida and in sheltered places further north. Vines arise as branches (long compound leaves) from underground widely creeping rhizomes that are slender, dark brown to black, and wiry that must be killed for eradication. Prior year's dead vines provide a trellis for reestablishment. Persists and colonizes by rhizomes, and spreads rapidly by wind-dispersed spores. The native American climbing fern [*L. palmatum* (Bernh.) Sw.] occurs in special habitats, does not have frilly foliage like Japanese climbing fern, and rarely forms extensive infestations except on rock cliffs.

Management strategies:
- Do not plant or use contaminated pine straw for mulch harvested from highly infested areas. Monitor areas where pine straw mulch has been used for seedling emergence. Control sprouts and seedlings. Bag and dispose of plants in a dumpster.
- Treat when new plants are young to prevent spore formation.
- Clean shoes, clothes, dogs, and equipment before leaving infested areas. Tiny spores can hitchhike, so extreme care must be used to prevent spread.
- Minimize disturbance within miles of where this plant occurs, and anticipate wider occupation when plants are present before disturbance.
- Burning treatments can worsen infestations and result in tree damage due to fire ladders.

Recommended control procedures:
- Thoroughly wet all leaves to as high as safe with a glyphosate herbicide as a 4-percent solution (1 pint per 3-gallon mix in water with a surfactant) directed at the fern to minimize nontarget damage (July to September before spore release).

Invasive Forbs

Forbs are broadleaf herbaceous plants that usually reproduce by seed and can be perennial with flattened stems on the ground and root crowns that persist over winter. Control treatments are usually by foliar sprays of herbicides. Persistent seeds in the soil and underground stems and rhizomes make control a lengthy and exacting process for eradication and rehabilitation.

Alligatorweed

Alligatorweed [*Alternanthera philoxeroides* (Mart.) Griseb.] is a perennial, evergreen forb with hollow round stems and opposite leaves at nodes. When erect, stems produce stalked white cloverlike flowers in upper axils during summer but no fruit or seeds. Horizontal stems readily branch and root at nodes in water to 6.5 feet (2 m) deep or when next to soil. Deep mats prevent other plants from germinating in the spring and overtop aquatic and upland plants, damaging wetland wildlife habitats. Grows in both fresh-to-slightly brackish waters. It spreads rapidly by stem fragments moved by water that root at nodes. Resembles other *Alternanthera* species, both nonnative and native, which have similar flowers, but none are stalked like alligatorweed. Also resembles the many knotweeds (*Polygonum* spp.) that inhabit wet soils and shorelines that have alternate leaves.

Management strategies:

- Alligator flea beetles (*Agasicles hygrophila* Selman & Vogt) have been used successfully to control alligatorweed where mean winter temperatures exceed 50 °F (10 °C).
- Minimize disturbance within miles of where this plant occurs, and anticipate wider occupation when plants are present before disturbance.
- Water-level management in reservoirs must be timed to accommodate herbicide applications, treatment progressions, and to minimize floating mats to prevent spread.

Recommended control procedures:

- Thoroughly wet all leaves with one of the following herbicides in water: to minimize impacts to nontarget plants, apply Garlon 4 (Renovate 3 for aquatic sites) or a glyphosate herbicide (Rodeo for aquatic sites) as a 2-percent solution (8 ounces per 3-gallon mix) for good control above the water line. Apply Habitat* as a 0.5-percent solution (2 ounces per 3-gallon mix) in a 100-gallon per-acre mix in spring to protect dormant native plants and to let them respond to release from alligatorweed or, when foliage is emerged, Clearcast* as a 1-percent solution (4 ounces per 3-gallon mix).

---

* Nontarget plants may be killed or injured by root uptake.

Big Blue Lilyturf, Creeping Liriope

   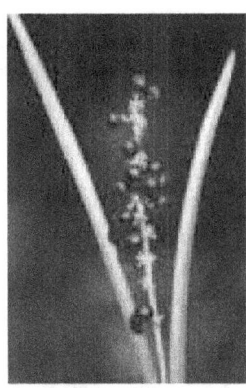

Big blue lilyturf [*Liriope muscari* (Decne.) L.H. Bailey] and creeping liriope [*L. spicata* (Thunb.) Lour.] are common ornamentals that form dense evergreen ground cover of crowded tufts of grasslike but thicker leaves, 6 to 18 inches (15 to 45 cm) high that increase with plant age. Stalked spikelike racemes of small lavender-to-lilac-to-white flowers jut upward in early summer to yield stalks of small green-to-black berrylike fruit in summer through winter. Both aggressively spread by radiating underground stems (rhizomes) that produce white plant initiates at nodes that remain interconnected for a time, and by seeds. Roots produce scattered small fleshy peanut-shaped corms that can sprout as well. Grow in full sun to shade and a range of soils, while spread is most rapid on moist highly organic soils. Many cultivars are sold and widely planted as ornamental ground cover and can escape to nearby forests by seeds.

Management strategies:

- Remove prior plantings, and control sprouts and seedlings. Bag and dispose of plants, underground corms, and fruit in a dumpster or burn.
- Treat when new plants are young to prevent seed formation.
- Pull, cut, and treat when fruit are not present.
- Frequent repeated mowing can assist control.

Recommended control procedures:

- Thoroughly wet leaves with one of the following herbicides in water with a surfactant (June to October with multiple applications to regrowth): a glyphosate herbicide as a 2-percent solution (8 ounces per 3-gallon mix), mix) or, when safety to surrounding plants is not a concern, Arsenal AC[*] as a 0.5 percent solution (2 ounces per 3-gallon mix), Arsenal PowerLine[*] as a 1-percent solution (4 ounces per 3-gallon mix), or Journey[*] as a 3-percent solution (12 ounces per 3-gallon mix) applied to actively growing shoots.

---

[*] Nontarget plants may be killed or injured by root uptake.

Chinese Lespedeza

 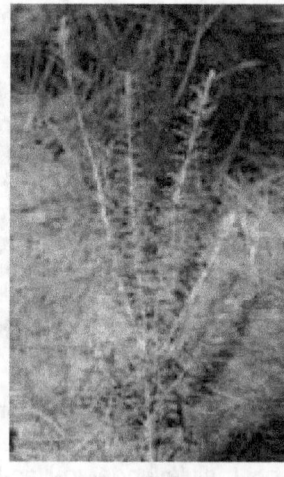  

Ted Bodner

Chinese lespedeza or sericea [*Lespedeza cuneata* (Dum. Cours.) G. Don] is a semiwoody upright leguminous forb to 6 feet (2 m) in height with many three-leaflet leaves feathered along erect slender whitish stems that often branch in the upper half. Many tiny cream-colored flowers in leaf axils during summer yield abundant single flat seeds in fall and winter. Plants remain standing dormant most of the winter and form dense stands that prevent forest regeneration and land access. Seed have low germination but are long lived in the soil seed bank and require long-term monitoring after control treatments. Seed spread by birds, ants, and rodents. Resembles native lespedeza [*L. virginica* (L.) Britton] which grows in tufted clumps instead of infestations, has crowded clusters of pink-purple to violet flowers, somewhat larger leaflets 0.6 to 1.2 inches (1.5 to 3 cm) long, and brown stems. Also resembles roundhead lespedeza (*L. capitata* Michx.), which has similar leaves but whitish flowers in round-topped clusters.

Management strategies:

- Do not plant. Remove prior plantings, and control sprouts and seedlings. Bag and dispose of fruit in a dumpster or burn.
- Pull, cut, and treat when seed are not present.
- Minimize disturbance within miles of where this plant occurs, and anticipate wider occupation when plants are present before disturbance.
- Manually pull when soil is moist to ensure removal of all roots.
- Prescribed burning can promote spread of the infestation margins and mowing will increase stem density and canopy cover.
- Suppressing can be accomplished by fertilization of nutrient poor soils.
- Sparingly eaten by most livestock when the plant is young and by goats when the plant is mature, while special varieties have been bred for livestock consumption.

Recommended control procedures:

- Thoroughly wet all foliage with one of the following herbicides in water with 0.25 to 0.50 percent surfactant from mid-June to late-July (before flowering): Garlon 4 as a 2-percent solution (8 ounces per 3-gallon mix) or a mixture of 1 ounce Vista XRT plus 1 ounce Garlon 4 per 3-gallon mix or for broadcast spraying, mix 6 to 12 ounces of Vista XRT and 1 quart of Garlon 4 Ultra per 100 gallons of water.
- Mowing 1 to 3 months before herbicide application can assist herbicide control.

Coltsfoot

Leslie Mehrhoff — Ohio State Weed Lab Archive — Leslie Mehrhoff — Chris Evans

Coltsfoot (*Tussilago farfara* L.) is an unusual low-growing perennial forb from thick branching underground white rhizomes to 10 feet (3 m) deep. Several dandelionlike flower heads per plant sprout in early spring on stout and bracted woolly haired stalks, then rosettes of colt-hoof shaped leaves appear after dandelionlike plumed seeds have dispersed throughout the growing season. Coltsfoot has the reverse growth sequence of most asters and can rapidly colonize on roadsides and disturbed lands, especially dry and droughty sites. Rhizomes and seeds can remain dormant in soil for long periods and are stimulated to germinate by disturbance.

Management strategies:
- Manually pull when first appears and when soil is moist to ensure removal of all rhizomes.
- Treat when new plants are young to prevent seed formation.

Recommended control procedures:
- Thoroughly wet all leaves with a glyphosate herbicide or Garlon 3A as a 2-percent solution (8 ounces per 3-gallon mix) in water with a surfactant. Treatments should be made in the summer when the leaves of coltsfoot are fully developed. Earlier applications can be used to stop seeding.

Crownvetch

Crownvetch [*Securigera varia* (L.) Lassen] (formerly *Coronilla varia* L.) is a deciduous perennial forb sprawling to form tangled mats to 3 feet (92 cm) high or scrambling over rocks, shrubs, and small trees. Feathery pinnately compound leaves [similar to true vetch species (*Vicia* spp.) but lacking tendrils], alternate on slender reclining stems. In summer a multitude of showy stemmed heads of white and pink flowers jut above entangled plants that yield tufts of slender seed pods in fall. One plant can cover 15 square feet (1.5 m^2) or more in a year from underground stems (rhizomes) with taproots. Forms brown, flattened patches in winter that resprout quickly in spring or remain green in southern areas. Seeds can germinate immediately after release, while viability in the soil seed bank is questioned. Persistent rhizomes sustain most patches and make control difficult. Crownvetch is planted on roadsides, surface mines, and in gardens and escapes into forest edges, openings, streamsides, and special habitats like rock outcroppings. It displaces plants and forms monocultures. Seed spread by wildlife and people while sediment-buried stems and rhizomes become established along streams.

Management strategies:

- Do not plant. Remove prior plantings, and control sprouts and seedlings. Bag and dispose of plants, rhizomes, and fruit in a dumpster or burn.
- Treat when new plants are young to prevent seed formation.
- Pull, cut, and treat when seed are not present.
- Repeated mowing can stop seed production.
- Minimize disturbance within miles of where this plant occurs, and anticipate wider occupation when plants are present before disturbance.
- Manually pull when soil is moist to ensure removal of all rhizomes.
- Readily eaten by most livestock, although reportedly toxic to horses.

Recommended control procedures:

- Thoroughly wet all leaves with a glyphosate herbicide or Garlon 3A as a 1- to 2-percent solution (4 to 8 ounces per 3-gallon mix) or Milestone VM[*] as a 0.5-percent solution (2 ounces per 3-gallon mix) in water with a surfactant during the vegetative stage prior to branching or during flowering. Apply Transline[*][†] as a 0.5-percent solution (2 ounces per 3-gallon mix); Arsenal AC[*] as a 0.5 percent solution (2 ounces per 3-gallon mix); or Arsenal PowerLine[*] as a 1-percent solution (4 ounces per 3-gallon mix) in fall, before frost or leaf drop.

---

[*] Nontarget plants may be killed or injured by root uptake.

[†] Transline controls a narrow spectrum of plant species.

Garlic Mustard

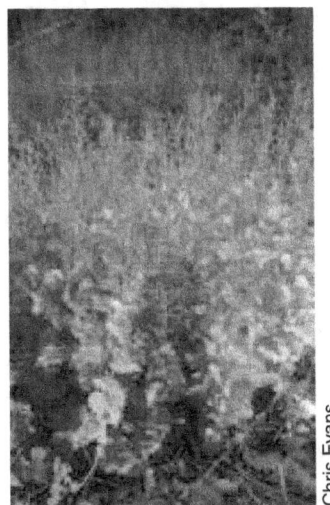

Garlic mustard [*Alliaria petiolata* (M. Bieb.) Cavara & Grande] is an upright cool-season biennial forb in small-to-extensive colonies under forest canopies, characterized by a faint-to-strong garlic odor from all parts of the plant when crushed (odor fades as fall approaches). It has basal rosettes of broadly arrow-point shaped leaves with wavy margins in the first year (remaining green during winter) and a 2- to 4-foot (60 to 120 cm) flower stalk and terminal clusters of flowers with four white petals in the second year. As a dead plant after June of the second year, it has long slender seed pods which ballistically disperse their seed up to 10 feet (3 m). Seed are spread by humans, animals, and water and can lie dormant for 2 to 6 years before germinating in spring. Stand density varies yearly depending on germination requirements of seeds in the soil seed bank, with a single crop germinating over a 2- to 4-year period.

Management strategies:
- Bag and dispose of plants and seed pods in a dumpster or burn.
- Treat when new plants are young to prevent seed formation.
- Pull, cut, and treat when seed pods are not present.
- Repeat cutting and mowing to prevent seeding.
- Minimize disturbance within miles of where this plant occurs, and anticipate wider occupation when plants are present before disturbance.
- Manually pull when soil is moist to ensure removal of all roots.
- Repeated annual prescribed burns in fall or early spring will control this plant, while "flaming" individual plants with propane torches has also shown preliminary success.
- Clean shoes, equipment, and vehicles to prevent seed dispersal.

Recommended control procedures:
- To control two generations, thoroughly wet all leaves with a glyphosate herbicide as a 2-percent solution in water (8 ounces per 3-gallon mix) when plant is bolting (April through June) or Garlon 4 as a 1- to 2-percent solution (4 to 8 ounces per 3-gallon mix) in water (March through May). Apply glyphosate in winter anytime the ground is not frozen or snow present to provide control and safety to dormant native plants. Include a surfactant or an aquatic surfactant when plants are near surface waters. For more selective control, apply Plateau[*] (see label) where permitted.

---

[*] Nontarget plants may be killed or injured by root uptake.

Nodding Plumeless Thistle, Musk Thistle

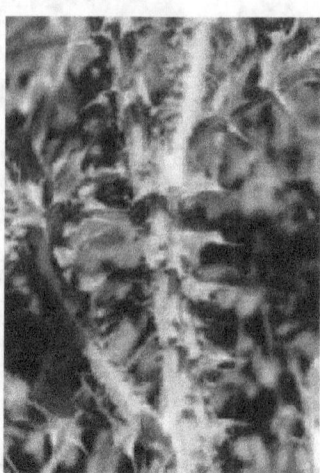

Jane Hargreaves

Nodding plumeless thistle (*Carduus nutans* L.) is a variable biennial or annual herb characterized by sharp spines on leaves, branching stems, bracts surrounding lavender flowers that sometimes nod to one side, thus, the common name, and plumed seed heads. Leafy rosettes first appear in spring or fall and form a deep, hollow taproot. Rosettes bolt within 6 months to 6 feet (2 m) high with midplant branches topped by one to a few composite flower heads that yield thousands of plumed seeds per plant. The plumes blow away on most, leaving the seed in the head, thus, the common name "plumeless." Spring seedlings can produce seeds in the same year while the more common fall rosettes overwinter to produce flower stalks the next spring. Seed dispersed by wind, water, livestock, human activity, and ants with viability exceeding 10 years in the soil. Most seed dispersed near the plant and with seed head fall. Rosettes also have axillary buds that produce sprouts when disturbed. Resembles the invasive bull thistle [*Cirsium vulgare* (Savi) Ten.] that has hairs on the upper leaf surfaces and the perennial Canada thistle [*C. arvense* (L.) Scop.] that has rhizomes, does not appear in the rosette form, and the flower/seed head bracts are not spiny except the most outer.

Management strategies:

- Bag and dispose of plants and seed heads in a dumpster or burn.
- Treat when new plants are young to prevent seed formation.
- Pull, cut, and treat when seeds are not present.
- Minimize disturbance within miles of where this plant occurs, and anticipate wider occupation when plants are present before disturbance.
- Manually pull when soil is moist to ensure removal of all roots.

Recommended control procedures:

- Thoroughly wet all leaves with one of the following herbicides in water with a surfactant: Transline[*][†] as a 0.5-percent solution (2 ounces per 3-gallon mix) applied during the rosette stage or prior to flowering, Garlon 3A or a glyphosate herbicide as a 2-percent solution (8 ounces per 3-gallon mix), Milestone VM[*] as a 0.5-percent solution (2 ounces per 3-gallon mix), or Overdrive®[*] as a 0.8-percent solution (0.3 ounce per 3 gallon mix) applied at the rosette growth stage.

---

[*] Nontarget plants may be killed or injured by root uptake.

[†] Transline controls a narrow spectrum of plant species.

Spotted Knapweed

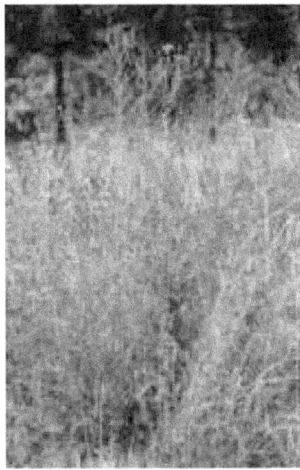

Steve Dewey

Spotted knapweed [*Centaurea stoebe* L. ssp. *micranthos* (Gugler) Hayek] is a bushy, winter-hardy plant. It is an erect-to-spreading perennial forb that lives 3 to 5 years and sometimes longer. A deep taproot supports an initial rosette of bluish-green, woolly, dandelionlike leaves. Stem leaves are pinnately dissected, becoming smaller and less dissected towards the tips of multiple woolly, hairy stems. Midplant branches are topped by a few to many pink-to-lavender thistle flowers constricted below the plume by distinctively fringed bracts with black tips, thus, the common name "spotted," to produce thousands of tiny bristle-topped seeds. Dead tops remain in winter and new sprouts appear in spring. Seeds are equipped for dispersal by wind, water, livestock, wildlife, and human activity with viability in the soil for many years. Seeds germinate throughout the growing season.

Management strategies:
- Bag and dispose of plants and seed heads in a dumpster or burn.
- Treat when new plants are young to prevent seed formation.
- Pull, cut, and treat when fruit are not present.
- Minimize disturbance within miles of where this plant occurs, and anticipate wider occupation when plants are present before disturbance.
- Manually pull when soil is moist to ensure removal of all roots.
- Prescribed burning is not recommended.

Recommended control procedures:
- Thoroughly wet all leaves with one of the following herbicides in water with a surfactant: Milestone VM[*] at 5 to 7 ounces per acre applied at the spring bolting or fall rosette stages; Tordon K[*][‡] at 0.25 to 0.5 pounds per acre will control spotted knapweed plants and seedlings for 2 to 3 years; Tordon K[*][‡] should be applied either in fall when the plants are in the rosette growth stage, or in spring during the bud-to-bloom stage; or Vanquish[*] at 1 to 2 pounds per acre (acid equivalent, see label). May require annual followup treatment for a minimum of 2 years; apply Overdrive[*] as a 0.2-percent solution (0.6 ounce per 3-gallon mix) plus Tordon 101[*][‡] as a 4-percent solution (2 pints per 3-gallon mix), or Garlon 3A as a 2- to 3-percent solution (8 to 12 ounces per 3-gallon mix) three to four times per year for 2 years.

[*] Nontarget plants may be killed or injured by root uptake.
[‡] When using Tordon herbicides, rainfall must occur within 6 days after application for needed soil activation. Tordon herbicides are restricted use pesticides.

Resource Information

Books

Burrrell, C.C. 2006. Native alternatives to invasive plants. Brooklyn, NY: Brooklyn Botanic Garden. 239 p.

Kaufman, S.R.; Kaufman, W.K. 2007. Invasive plants: a guide to identification, impacts, and control of common North American species. Mechanicsburg, PA: Stackpole Books. 458 p.

Langeland, K.A.; Cherry, H.M.; McCormick, C.M.; Craddock Burks, K.A., eds. 2008. Identification & biology of nonnative plants in Florida's natural areas. Gainesville, FL: University of Florida. 193 p.

Randall, J.M.; Marinelli, J., eds. 1996. Invasive plants: weeds of the global garden. Handb. 149. Brooklyn, NY: Brooklyn Botanic Garden. 111 p.

Manuals

Evans, C.W.; Moorhead, D.J.; Bargeron, C.T.; Douce, G.K. 2006. Invasive plant responses to silvicultural practices in the South. BW–2006–03. Tifton, GA: The University of Georgia, Bugwood Network. 52 p.

Kaeser, M.J.; Kirkman, L.K. 2010. Field and restoration guide to common native warm-season grasses of the longleaf pine ecosystem. Newton, GA, Joseph W. Jones Ecological Research Center at Ichauway. 71 p.

Langeland, K.A.; Stocker, R.K., eds. 2009. Control of nonnative plants in natural areas of Florida. SP–242. Gainesville, FL: University of Florida, Institute of Food and Agricultural Sciences. 31 p. http://edis.ifas.ufl.edu/pdffiles/WG/WG20900.pdf. [Date accessed: August 28].

Smith, Tim E., ed. 1993. Missouri vegetation management manual. Jefferson City, MO: Missouri Department of Conservation, Natural History Division. 148 p.

Swearingen, J.; Reshetiloff, K.; Slattery, B.; Zwicker, S. 2002. Plant invaders of Mid-Atlantic natural areas. Washington, DC: U.S. Department of the Interior, National Park Service and U.S. Fish and Wildlife Service. 82 p.

Tennessee Exotic Pest Plant Council. 1996. Tennessee exotic plant management manual. Nashville, TN: Tennessee Exotic Pest Plant Council, Warner Parks Nature Center. 118 p.

Tu, M.; Hurd, C.; Randall, J.M., eds. 2001. Weed control methods handbook: tools and techniques for use in natural areas. The Nature Conservancy. http://www.invasive.org/gist/handbook.html. [Date accessed: August 28, 2009].

Articles and Reports

Allen, S.L.; Hepp, G.R.; Miller, J.H. 2007. Use of herbicides to control alligatorweed and restore native plants in managed marshes. Wetlands. 37: 739–748.

Brandon, A.L.; Gibson, D.J.; Middleton, B.A. 2004. Mechanisms for dominance in an early successional old field by the invasive non-native *Lespedeza cueata* (Dum. Cours.) G. Don. Biological Invasions. 6: 483–493.

Blair, M.P. 2008. Herbicide and application options for Amur (bush) honeysuckle. Southern Weed Science Society Annual Meeting Proceedings. 61: 1–4.

Britton, K.O.; Duerr, D.A., II; Miller, J.H. 2005. Understanding and controlling nonnative forest pests in the South. In: Rauscher, H. Michael; Johnson, Kurt, eds. Southern forest science: past, present, and future. Gen. Tech. Rep. SRS-75. Asheville, NC: U.S. Department of Agriculture Forest Service, Southern Research Station: 133–154. Chapter 14.

continued

Resource Information (continued)

Articles and Reports (continued)

Bruce, K.A.; Cameron, G.N.; Harcombe, P.A.; Jubinsky, G. 1997. Introduction, impact on native habitats, and management of a woody invader, the Chinese tallow-tree, *Sapium sebiferum* (L.) Roxb. Natural Areas Journal. 17: 255–260.

Call, N.M.; Coble, H.D.; Perez-Fernandez, T. 2000. Tropical soda apple (*Solanum viarum*) herbicide susceptibility and competitiveness in tall fescue (*Festuca arundinacea*). Weed Technology. 14: 252–260.

Capo-chichi, L.J.A; Faircloth, W.H.; Williamson, A.G.; Patterson, M.G.; Miller, J.H.; van Santen, E. 2008. Invasion dynamics and genotypic diversity of cogongrass (*Imperata cylindrica*) at the point of introduction in the Southeastern United States. Invasive Plant Science and Management. 1:133–141.

Carlson, A.M.; Grochov, D.L. 2004. Effects of herbicide on the invasive biennial *Alliaria petiolata* (garlic mustard) and initial responses of native plants in a southwestern Ohio forest. Restoration Ecology. 12:559– 567.

Culley, T.M.; Hardiman, N.A. 2007. The beginning of a new invasive plant: a history of the ornamental callery pear in the United States. BioScience. 57: 956–964.

DeMeester, J.E.; Richter, D. D. 2009. Restoring restoration; removal of the invasive plant *Microstegium vimineum* from a North Carolina wetland. Biological Invasions. Published online June 12, 2009. http://www.springerlink.com/content/86x34u9176436025/ [Date accessed: December 14, 2009].

Demers, C.; Long, A. 2002. Controlling invasive exotic plants in north Florida forests. Ext. Publ. SS–FOR–19. Gainesville, FL: University of Florida, Agronomy Department, Institute of Food and Agricultural Sciences. 9 p. http://edis.ifas.ufl.edu/. [Date accessed: April 20, 2005].

Derr, J.F. 1989. Multiflora rose (*Rosa multiflora*) control with metsulfuron. Weed Technology. 3: 381–384.

Dickens, R.; Buchanan, G.A. 1975. Control of cogongrass with herbicides. Weed Science. 23:194–197.

DiTomaso, J.M.; Kyser, G.B. 2007. Control of *Ailanthus altissima* using stem herbicide application techniques. Arboriculture & Urban Forestry. 33: 55–63.

Donahue, C.; Rogers, W.E.; Siemann, E. 2006. Restoring an invaded prairie by mulching live *Sapium sebiferum* (Chinese tallow trees): effects of mulch on *Sapium* seed germination. Natural Areas Journal. 26: 244–253.

Dozier, H.; Gaffney, J.J.; McDonald, S.K.; Johnson, E.R.R.L.; Shilling, D.G. 1998. Cogongrass in the United States: history, ecology, impacts, and management. Weed Technology. 12:737–743.

Dreyer, G.D. 1988. Efficacy of triclopyr in rootkilling oriental bittersweet (*Celastrus orbiculata* Thunb.) and certain other woody weeds. Northeast Weed Science Society Annual Meeting Proceedings. 42: 120–121.

Edgin, B.; Ebinger, J.E. 2001. Control of autumn olive (*Elaeagnus umbellata* Thunb.) at Beall Woods Nature Preserve, Illinois, USA. Natural Areas Journal. 21: 386–388.

Edwards, M.B.; Gonzalez, F.E. 1986. Forestry herbicide control of kudzu and Japanese honeysuckle in loblolly pine sites in central Georgia. Southern Weed Science Society Annual Meeting Proceedings. 39: 272–275.

Everest, J.W.; Miller, J.H.; Ball, D.M.; Patterson, M. 1999. Kudzu in Alabama: history, uses, and control. ANR–65. Auburn, AL: Alabama Cooperative Extension. 6 p.

Faircloth, W. H.; Patterson, M.G.; Teem, D.H.; Miller, J.H. 2003. Cogongrass (*Imperata cylindrica*): management tactics on rights-of-way. Southern Weed Science Society Annual Meeting Proceedings. 55:162.

continued

Resource Information (continued)

Articles and Reports (continued)

Ferrell, J.A.; Mullahey, J.J.; Langeland, K.A.; Kline, W.N. 2006. Control of tropical soda apple (*Solanum viarum*) with aminopyralid. Weed Technology. 20: 453–457.

Flory, S.L.; Clay, K. 2009. Invasive plant removal methods determines native plant community responses. Journal of Applied Ecology. 46: 434–442.

Flory, S.L. 2010. Management of *Microtegium vimineum* invasions and recovery of resident plant communities. Restoration Ecology. 18:103–112.

Frey, M.N.; Herms, C.P.; Cardina, J. 2007. Cold weather applications of glyphosate for garlic mustard (*Alliaria petiolata*) control. Weed Technology. 21: 656–660.

Gan, J.; Miller, J. H.; Wang, H.; Taylor, J. W. 2009. Invasion of tallow tree in the Southern U. S. forests: influencing factors and implications for mitigation. Canadian Journal Forest Research. 39: 1346–1356.

Gioeli, K.; Langeland, K. 2006. Brazilian pepper-tree control. Ext. Publ. SS–AGR–17. Gainesville, FL: University of Florida, Agronomy Department, Institute of Food and Agricultural Sciences. 7 p. http://edis.ifas.ufl.edu/AA219. [Date accessed: April 27, 2007].

Glasgow, L.S.; Matlack, G.R. 2006. The effects of prescribed burning and canopy openness on establishment of two non-native plant species in a deciduous forest, southeast Ohio, USA. Forest Ecology and Management. 238: 319–329.

Harrington, T.B.; Miller, J.H. 2005. Effects of application rate, timing, and formulation of glyphosate and triclopyr on control of Chinese privet (*Ligustrum sinense*). Weed Technology. 19: 47–54.

Johnson, J; Griffin, S; Taylor, J. Aerial glyphosate application to control privet in mature hardwood stands. Macon, GA, Georgia Forestry Commission, http://www.gatrees.org/ForestManagement/documents/AerialGlyphosateApplicationtoControlPrivet2009.pdf [Date accessed: February 2, 2010].

Jose, S.; Cox, J.; Miller, D.L.; Shilling, D.G.; Merritt, S. 2002. Alien plant invasions: the story of cogongrass in southeastern forests. Journal of Forestry. 100:41–44.

Judge, C.A.; Neal, J.C.; Derr, J.F. 2005. Response of Japanese stiltgrass (*Microstegium vimineum*) to application timing, rate, and frequency of postemergence herbicides. Weed Technology. 19: 912–917.

King, S.E.; Grace, J.B. 2000. The effects of soil flooding on the establishment of cogongrass (*Imperata cylindrica*), a nonindigenous invader of the Southeastern United States. Wetlands. 20:300–306.

Klepac, J.; Rummer, R.B.; Hanula, J.L.; Horn, S. 2007. Mechanical removal of Chinese privet. Res. Pap. SRS–43. Asheville, NC: U.S. Department of Agriculture Forest Service, Southern Research Station. 5 p.

Kline, W.N.; Duquesnel, J.G. 1996. Control of problem vegetation: a key to ecosystem management. Down to Earth. 51: 20–28.

Koger, C.H.;Stritzke, J.F; Cummings, D.C. 2002. Control of sericea lespedeza (*Lespedeza cuneata*) with triclopyr, fluroxypyr, and metsulfuron. Weed Technology. 16:893-900.

Loewenstein, N.J.; Miller J.H, eds. 2007. Proceedings of the regional cogongrass conference: a cogongrass management guide. Auburn University, AL: Alabama Cooperative Extension System. 77 p. http://www.cogongrass.org/conference.cfm. [Date accessed: February 4, 2010].

continued

Resource Information (continued)

Articles and Reports (continued)

Love, J.P.; Anderson, J.T. 2009. Seasonal effects of four control methods on the invasive Morrow's honeysuckle (*Lonicera morrowii*) and initial responses of understory plants in a southwestern Pennsylvania old field. Restoration Ecology. 17: 549–559.

MacDonald, G.E. 2004. Cogongrass (*Imperata cylindrica*) – biology, ecology, and management. Critical Reviews in Plant Science. 23:367–380.

Miller, J.H.; Edwards, Boyd. 1983. Kudzu: where did it come from? And how can we stop it? Southern Journal of Applied Forestry. 7: 165–169.

Miller, J.H. 1985. Testing herbicides for kudzu eradication on a Piedmont site. Southern Journal of Applied Forestry. 9: 128–132.

Miller, J.H. 1986. Kudzu eradication trials testing fifteen herbicides. Southern Weed Science Society Annual Meeting Proceedings. 39: 276–281.

Miller, J.H. 1988. Kudzu eradication trials with new herbicides. Southern Weed Science Society Annual Meeting Proceedings. 41: 220–225.

Miller, James H. 1998. Exotic invasive plants in southeastern forests. In: Britton, K.O., ed. Proceedings of the exotic pests of eastern forests. Nashville, TN: Exotic Pest Plant Council: 97–105.

Miller, James H. 1998. Primary screening of forestry herbicides for control of Chinese privet (*Ligustrum sinense*), Chinese wisteria (*Wisteria sinensis*), and trumpetcreeper (*Campsis radicans*). Southern Weed Science Society Annual Meeting Proceedings. 51: 161–162.

Miller, James H. 2000. Refining rates and treatment sequences for cogongrass (*Imperata cylindrica*) control with imazapyr and glyphosate. Southern Weed Science Society Annual Meeting Proceedings. 53: 181.

Miller, J.H.; Schelhas, J. 2008. Adaptive collaborative restoration: a key concept for invasive plant management. In: Kohli, R.K.; Singh, J.P.; Batish, D.R.; Jose, S., eds. Invasive plants and forest ecosystems. Boca Raton, FL: CRC Press: 251–265. Chapter 15.

Mueller, T.C.; Robinson, D.K.; Beeler, J.E. [and others]. 2003. *Dioscorea oppositifolia* L. phenotypic evaluations and comparison of control strategies. Weed Technology. 17: 705–710.

Mullahey, J.J.; Colvin, D.L. 2000. Weeds in the sunshine: tropical soda apple (*Solanum viarum*) in Florida–1999. Gainesville, FL: University of Florida, Institute of Food and Agricultural Sciences. 7 p.

Neal, J.C.; Skroch, W.A. 1985. Effects of timing and rate of glyphosate application on toxicity to selected woody ornamentals. Journal of American Society of Horticultural Science. 110: 860–864.

Nuzzo, V.A. 1991. Experimental control of garlic mustard (*Alliaria petiolata* (Bieb.) Cavara & Grande) in northern Illinois using fire, herbicide, and cutting. Natural Areas Journal. 11: 158–167.

Pergrams, O.R.W.; Norton, J.E. 2006. Treating a single stem can kill whole shrub: a scientific assessment of buckthorn control methods. Natural Areas Journal. 26: 300–309.

Rathfon, R.; Ruble, K. 2007. Herbicide treatments for controlling invasive bush honeysuckle in a mature hardwood forest in west-central Indiana. In: Buckley, David S.; Clatterbuck, Wayne K., eds. Proceedings, 15th central hardwood forest conference. e-Gen. Tech. Rep. SRS-101. Asheville, NC: U.S. Department of Agriculture Forest Service, Southern Research Station: 187–197.

continued

Resource Information (continued)

Articles and Reports (continued)

Regehr, D.; Frey, D.R. 1988. Selective control of Japanese honeysuckle (*Lonicera japonica*). Weed Technology. 2: 139–143.

Shaw, D.R.; Arnold, J.C. 2002. Weed control from herbicide combinations with glyphosate. Weed Technology. 16: 1–6.

Solodar, J. 2006. A method for control of *Euonymus fortunei* using Roundup Pro (glyphostate). Missouriensis. 26: 1–6.

Szafoni, R.E. 1991. Vegetation management guidelines: multiflora rose (*Rosa multiflora* Thunb.). Natural Areas Journal. 11: 215–216.

Thomas, L.K., Jr. 1993. Chemical grubbing for control of exotic wisteria. Castanea. 58: 209–213.

Underwood, J.F.; Sperow, C.B., Jr. 1985. Control methods for multiflora rose (*Rosa multiflora* Thunb.) with metsulfuron methyl. North Central Weed Science Society Annual Meeting Proceedings. 40: 59–63.

Washburn, B.E.; Barnes, T.G. 2000. Postemergence tall fescue (*Festuca arundinacea*) control at different growth stages with glyphosate and AC 263,222. Weed Technology. 14: 223–230.

Washburn, T.G.; Washburn, B. 2001. Controlling tall fescue, common Bermuda, and bahia grass. Wildland Weeds. 4: 5–8.

Willard, T.R.; Gaffney, J.F.; Shilling, D.G. 1997. Influence of herbicide combinations and application technology on cogongrass (*Imperata cylindrica*) control. Weed Technology. 11: 76–80.

Willard, T. R.; Shilling, D.G. 1990. The influence of growth stage and mowing on competition between *Paspalum notatum* and *Imperata cylindrica*. Tropical Grasslands. 24:81–86.

Willard, T. R., Hall, D.H.; Shilling, D.G.; Lewis, J.H.; Currey, W.L. 1990. Cogongrass (*Imperata cylindrica*) distribution on Florida highway rights-of-way. Weed Technology. 4:658–660.

Willard, T.R.; Shilling, D.G.; Gaffney, J.F.; Currey, W.L. 1996. Mechanical and chemical control of cogongrass (*Imperata cylindrica*). Weed Technology. 10:722-726.

Wright, R.S.; Byrd, J.D., Jr. 2008. Effective herbicides for control of mimosa (*Albizia julibrissin*). Southern Weed Science Society Annual Meeting Proceedings. 61: 175.

Yeiser, J.L. 1999. Japanese honeysuckle control in a minor hardwood bottom of southwest Arkansas. Southern Weed Science Society Annual Meeting Proceedings. 52: 108–111.

Zeller, M.; Leslie, D. 2004. Japanese climbing fern control trials in planted pine. Wildland Weeds. 7: 6, 8–9.

Magazine

Florida Exotic Plant Pest Council and Southeast Exotic Pest Plant Council. 1996–2013. Wildland Weeds. Gainesville, FL. Quarterly.

continued

Resource Information (continued)

Web Sites

Global

Global Invasive Species Database: http://www.issg.org/database/welcome/

The Nature Conservancy's Global Invasive Species Team: http://www.invasive.org/gist/index.html

An International Nonindigenous Species Database Network: http://www.nisbase.org/nisbase/index.jsp

National

Center for Invasive Species and Ecosystem Health: http://www.bugwood.org/index.cfm

CDMS Source for herbicide labels and MSDS sheets: http://www.cdms.net/LabelsMsds/LMDefault.aspx?t=

Institute for Biological Invasion: http://invasions.bio.utk.edu/Default.htm

Invasive and Exotic Species (Invasive.org): http://www.invasive.org/

Invasive Plants Control Webinars: http://www.ipcwebsolutions.com/index.htm

Invasive Plants of the United States: Identification, Biology, and Control: http://www.invasive.org/weedcd/

National Association of Exotic Pest Plant Councils: http://www.naeppc.org/

NatureServe: http://www.natureserve.org/explorer/

Federal Government Agencies

Alien Plant Invaders of Natural Areas (PCA, National Park Service): http://www.nps.gov/plants/alien/factmain.htm

Animal and Plant Health Inspection Service (APHIS):
    http://www.aphis.usda.gov/plant_health/plant_pest_info/weeds/index.shtml

Aquatic Nuisance Species Task Force (ANS): http://www.anstaskforce.gov/default.php

Agricultural Research Service: The Exotic and Invasive Weeds Research Unit:
    http://www.ars.usda.gov/main/site_main.htm?modecode=53-25-43-00

Cooperative State Research, Education, and Extension Service (CSREES) Invasive Species (USDA Cooperative Extension Service): http://www.csrees.usda.gov/invasivespecies.cfm

National Institute of Invasive Species Science: http://www.niiss.org/cwis438/websites/niiss/About.php?WebSiteID=1

National Biological Information Infrastructure (NBII) Invasive Species Information Node:
    http://invasivespecies.net/default_008.html

PLANTS National Database: http://plants.usda.gov/

Southern Region Forest Service Forest Inventory and Analysis Invasive Plants: http://srsfia2.fs.fed.us/SNIPET/

U.S. National Arboretum: http://www.usna.usda.gov/Gardens/invasives.html

U.S. Army Environmental Center (USAEC) Pest Management: http://el.erdc.usace.army.mil/pmis/

continued

Resource Information (continued)

Web Sites (continued)

Federal Government Agencies (continued)

U.S. Fish and Wildlife Service Invasive Species Program: http://www.fws.gov/invasives/

USDA Agricultural Research Service (ARS) Invaders Database System: http://invader.dbs.umt.edu/Noxious_Weeds/

USDA National Invasive Species Information Center: http://www.invasivespeciesinfo.gov/

USDA Forest Service Fire Effects Information System: http://www.fs.fed.us/database/feis/

USDA Forest Service Invasive Species Program: http://www.fs.fed.us/invasivespecies/index.shtml

USDA Forest Service: http://www.fs.fed.us/foresthealth/programs/invasive_species_mgmt.shtml

U.S. Environmental Protection Agency Invasive Species Program: http://www.epa.gov/owow/invasive_species/

Weeds Gone Wild: Alien Plant Invaders of Natural Areas: http://www.nps.gov/plants/alien/

Regional

Cogongrass Web site, The University of Georgia: http://www.cogongrass.org

Flora of the Southeast: http://www.herbarium.unc.edu/seflora/species.htm

Invasive Plant Atlas of the MidSouth: http://www.gri.msstate.edu/ipams/

Invasive Plant Atlas of New England: http://www.eddmaps.org/ipane/

Invasive Plants of the Thirteen Southeastern States: http://www.invasive.org/south/seweedsnew.cfm

Mid-Atlantic Exotic Pest Plant Council: http://www.ma-eppc.org/

Mid-West Invasive Plant Network: http://mipn.org/

Southeast Exotic Pest Plant Council: http://www.se-eppc.org/

USDA Forest Service Invasive Species of the South: http://www.invasive.org/south/

State

Alabama Forestry Commission Invasive Plants: http://www.forestry.alabama.gov/

Exotic Plants of North Carolina: http://www.ncdot.org/doh/preconstruct/pe/neu/NEUProcedures/NCDOT_Invasive_Exotic_Plants.pdf

National Association of State Departments of Agriculture (NASDA): http://www.nasda.org/

State Exotic Pest Plant Councils: http://www.naeppc.org/

State Laws and Regulations: http://www.invasivespeciesinfo.gov/laws/statelaws.shtml

Texasinvasive.org: http://www.texasinvasives.org/

Appendix A—Nonnative Invasive Plant Species Not to be Used or Recommended for Ornamental, Landscapes, Food/Herbal Plantings, or Water Gardens

Most of the southern plant invasions have started from escaped ornamental plantings that have occurred over 400 years and continue today. The increasing deluge of aquatic invasive plants destroying native communities that inhabit our natural waters and wetlands are coming from those used and discarded from home water gardens. Homeowners are free to plant and "over the fence" discard a full range of commercially available plants without regard to their invasiveness unless restricted by local, State, and Federal regulations (mainly focused on agricultural pest introductions) or community covenants. Some, like English ivy, silverthorn, Bradford pear, and silver plumegrass are even required by some subdivision covenants. Many of these escaped ornamentals are now widely recognized and listed as invasive species, but consumers are unaware or complacent of the real dangers they pose to natural communities as they replace our native plants. Invasive plant species are still frequently recommended in State horticultural extension bulletins and manuals. The threat is worsened as both traditional and new invasive plant species are mass produced by the plant industry and sold through large and small outlets that are essentially insulated from the current knowledge of the incurred societal costs. Landscape architects have been trained to select invasive plants for creating ornamental and horticultural landscapes with repeated composition and plant forms with little or no understanding of the greater consequences. Other invasive plants can be bought through the Internet, especially those used in oriental cooking and herbal mixtures. The most aware and bothered public are those that must persistently fight back invasive plants taking over their properties and parks plagued by unwise planting choices by neighbors, communities, cities, and highway departments.

This is a "do not plant" list of invasive ornamental (and some oriental food and herbal) plants recognized and listed by State and Federal Agencies and exotic pest plant councils. As a good neighbor and land steward, please do not plant these plants and remove any that already exist from your property. Even a small number of plants can cause eventual destruction to the healthy surrounding plant communities and their environment. Wind, water, birds, and mammals are perpetually transporting ornamental invasive plant parts, fruit, and seed throughout the urban, suburban, and rural landscapes. These escaped plants move outward to invade surrounding lands and waterways. With your individual invasive plant management efforts and conscientious use of noninvasive plants in your landscape, we can assure a better future for coming generations. Please ask ornamental plant growers and outlets not to grow or sell these plants. It is recognized that seed viability can vary by cultivar and populations, while hybridization can result in increased viability.

Invasive Trees

Do Not Plant These Invasive Trees

Amur maple	*Acer ginnala* Maxim.
Norway maple	*Acer platanoides* L.
Sycamore maple	*Acer pseudoplatanus* L.
Tree-of-heaven	*Ailanthus altissima* (Mill.) Swingle
Silktree, mimosa	*Albizia julibrissin* Durazz.
Paper mulberry	*Broussonetia papyrifera* (L.) L'Hér. ex Vent.
Camphortree	*Cinnamomum camphora* (L.) J. Presl
Australian pine, sheoak (all species)	*Casuarina* spp. Rumph. ex L.
Russian olive	*Elaeagnus angustifolia* L.
Chinese parasoltree	*Firmiana simplex* (L.) W. Wight
Glossy buckthorn	*Frangula alnus* Mill.
Melaleuca, paperbark	*Melaleuca quinquenervia* (Cav.) S.F. Blake
Chinaberrytree	*Melia azedarach* L.
White mulberry	*Morus alba* L.
Princesstree, paulownia	*Paulownia tomentosa* (Thunb.) Siebold & Zucc. ex Steud.
Japanese black pine	*Pinus thunbergii* Parl.
Hardy orange	*Poncirus trifoliata* (L.) Raf.

continued

Appendix A—Nonnative Invasive Plant Species Not to be Used or Recommended for Ornamental, Landscapes, Food/Herbal Plantings, or Water Gardens (continued)

Invasive Trees (continued)

Do Not Plant These Invasive Trees (continued)

White poplar	*Populus alba* L.
Callery pear, Bradford pear	*Pyrus calleryana* Decne.
Common buckthorn	*Rhamnus cathartica* L.
Rose myrtle	*Rhodomyrtus tomentosus* (Aiton) Hassk
Octopus tree, schefflera	*Schefflera actinophylla* (Endl.) Harms
Peruvian peppertree	*Schinus molle* L.
Brazilian peppertree	*Schinus terebinthifolius* Raddi
Java plum	*Syzygium cumini* (L.) Skeels
Tamarisk (all species)	*Tamarix* spp. L.
Tallowtree, popcorntree	*Triadica sebifera* (L.) Small
Siberian elm	*Ulmus pumila* L.
Tungoil tree	*Vernicia fordii* (Hemsl.) Airy-Shaw
Common jujube	*Ziziphus zizyphus* (L.) Karst.

Invasive Shrubs

Do Not Plant These Invasive Shrubs

Japanese barberry	*Berberis thunbergii* DC.
Common barberry	*Berberis vulgaris* L.
Butterflybush	*Buddleja davidii* Franch.
Scotch broom	*Cytisus scoparius* (L.) Link
Silverthorn, thorny olive	*Elaeagnus pungens* Thunb.
Autumn olive	*Elaeagnus umbellata* Thunb.
Winged burning bush	*Euonymus alatus* (Thunb.) Seibold
Chinese holly	*Ilex cornuta* Lindl. & Paxton
Japanese holly	*Ilex crenata* Thunb.
Lantana	*Lantana camara* L.
Shrubby or bicolor lespedeza	*Lespedeza bicolor* Turcz.
Thunberg's lespedeza	*Lespedeza thunbergii* (DC.) Nakai
Japanese privet	*Ligustrum japonicum* Thunb.
Glossy privet	*Ligustrum lucidum* W.T. Aiton
Border privet	*Ligustrum obtusifolium* Siebold & Zucc.
California privet	*Ligustrum ovalifolium* Hassk.
Chinese privet	*Ligustrum sinense* Lour.
European privet	*Ligustrum vulgare* L.
Bell's honeysuckle	*Lonicera* × *bella* Zabel [*morrowii* × *tatarica*]
Sweet breath of spring	*Lonicera fragrantissima* Lindl. & Paxton
Amur honeysuckle	*Lonicera maackii* (Rupr.) Herder
Morrow's honeysuckle	*Lonicera morrowi* A. Gray
Tatarian honeysuckle	*Lonicera tatarica* L.
Dwarf honeysuckle	*Lonicera xylosteum* L.
Leatherleaf mahonia	*Mahonia bealei* (Fortune) Carrière

continued

Appendix A—Nonnative Invasive Plant Species Not to be Used or Recommended for Ornamental, Landscapes, Food/Herbal Plantings, or Water Gardens (continued)

Invasive Shrubs (continued)

Do Not Plant These Invasive Shrubs (continued)

Sacred bamboo, nandina	*Nandina domestica* Thunb.
Strawberry guava	*Psidium cattleianum* Sabine
Japanese knotweed	*Polygonum cuspidatum* Siebold & Zucc.
Common pear	*Pyrus communis* L.
Castorbean	*Ricinus communis* L.
Macartney rose	*Rosa bracteata* J. C. Wendl.
Cherokee rose	*Rosa laevigata* Michx.
Multiflora rose	*Rosa multiflora* Thunb.
Rugosa rose	*Rosa rugosa* Thunb.
Himalayan blackberry	*Rubus armeniacus* Focke
Wine raspberry	*Rubus phoenicolasius* Maxim.
Japanese meadowsweet	*Spiraea japonica* L. f.
Common gorse	*Ulex europaeus* L.
Linden arrowwood	*Viburnum dilatatum* Thunb.

Invasive Vines

Do Not Plant These Invasive Vines

Five-leaf akebia, chocolate vine	*Akebia quinata* (Houtt.) Decne.
Amur peppervine, porcelain berry	*Ampelopsis brevipedunculata* (Maxim.) Trautv.
Bushkiller	*Cayratia japonica* (Thunb.) Gagnep.
Oriental bittersweet	*Celastrus orbiculatus* Thunb.
Sweet autumn virginsbower	*Clematis terniflora* DC.
Winged yam	*Dioscorea alata* L.
Air-potato	*Dioscorea bulbifera* L.
Chinese yam	*Dioscorea oppositifolia* L.
Winter creeper	*Euonymus fortunei* (Turcz.) Hand.-Maz.
Ground ivy, creeping charlie	*Glechoma hederacea* L.
Japanese hop	*Humulus japonicus* Siebold & Zucc.
Swamp morning-glory	*Ipomoea aquatica* Forssk.
Gloria de la manana, shrub morning-glory	*Ipomoea carnea* ssp. *fistulosa* (Mart. ex Choisy) D. Austin
Redstar, red morning-glory	*Ipomoea coccinea* L.
Ivyleaf morning-glory	*Ipomoea hederacea* Jacq.
Japanese honeysuckle	*Lonicera japonica* Thunb.
Colchis ivy or Persian ivy	*Hedera colchica* (K. Koch) K. Koch.
English ivy	*Hedera helix* L.
Atlantic Ivy or Irish ivy	*Hedera hibernica* (G. Kirchn.) Bean
Catclawvine	*Macfadyena unguis-cati* (L.) A.H. Gentry
Skunk vine	*Paederia foetida* L.
Chinese wisteria	*Wisteria sinensis* (Sims) DC.
Japanese wisteria	*Wisteria floribunda* (Willd.) DC.
Common periwinkle	*Vinca minor* L. (vegetative spread)
Bigleaf periwinkle	*Vinca major* L. (vegetative spread)

continued

Appendix A—Nonnative Invasive Plant Species Not to be Used or Recommended for Ornamental, Landscapes, Food/Herbal Plantings, or Water Gardens (continued)

Invasive Grasses and Canes

Do Not Plant These Invasive Grasses and Canes

Giant reed	*Arundo donax* L. (vegetative spread)
Black bamboo	*Bambusa* spp. Schreb.
Uruguayan pampas grass	*Cortaderia selloana* (Schult. & Schult. f.) Asch. & Graebn.
Weeping lovegrass	*Eragrostis curvula* (Schrad.) Nees
Japanese bloodgrass, Red Baron grass	*Imperata cylindrica* (L.) P. Beauv.
Chinese silvergrass	*Miscanthus sinensis* Andersson
Crimson fountaingrass	*Pennisetum setaceum* (Forssk.) Chiov.
Golden bamboo	*Phyllostachys aurea* Carrière ex A. Rivière & C. Rivière

Invasive Ferns

Do Not Plant These Invasive Ferns

Japanese climbing fern	*Lygodium japonicum* (Thunb.) Sw.
Small-leaf climbing fern	*Lygodium microphyllum* (Cav.) R. Br.
Narrow swordfern, Boston fern	*Nephrolepis cordifolia* (L.) C. Presl

Invasive Forbs

Do Not Plant These Invasive Forbs

Corn cockle	*Agrostemma githago* L.
Garlic mustard	*Alliaria petiolata* (M. Bieb.) Cavara & Grande
Coco yam, elephant's ears	*Colocasia esculenta* (L.) Schott
Queen Anne's lace, wild carrot	*Daucus carota* L.
Orange daylily	*Hemerocallis fulva* (L.) L.
Ornamental jewelweed	*Impatiens glandulifera* Royle
Yellow flag iris	*Iris pseudacorus* L.
Chinese lespedeza, serecia	*Lespedeza cuneata* (Dum. Cours.) G. Don
Big blue lilyturf	*Liriope muscari* (Decne.) L.H. Bailey
Creeping liriope	*Liriope spicata* (Thunb.) Lour.
Purple loosestrife	*Lythrum salicaria* L.
Crownvetch	*Securigera varia* (L.) Lassen

Invasive Aquatic Plants

Do Not Plant or Release into Natural Waters These Invasive Aquatic Plants

Alligatorweed	*Alternanthera philoxeroides* (Mart.) Griseb.
Feathered mosquitofern	*Azolla pinnata* R. Br.
Brazilian waterhyssop	*Bacopa egensis* (Poepp.) Pennell
Pond water-starwort	*Callitriche stagnalis* Scop.
Watersprite	*Ceratopteris thalictroides* (L.) Brongn.
Beckett's water trumpet	*Cryptocoryne beckettii* Thwaites ex Trimen.

continued

Appendix A—Nonnative Invasive Plant Species Not to be Used or Recommended for Ornamental, Landscapes, Food/Herbal Plantings, or Water Gardens (continued)

Aquatic Plants (continued)

Do Not Plant or Release into Natural Waters These Invasive Aquatic Plants (continued)

Brazilian waterweed	*Egeria densa* Planch.
Common water hyacinth	*Eichhornia crassipes* (Mart.) Solms
Waterthyme, hydrilla	*Hydrilla verticillata* (L. f.) Royle
Water-poppy	*Hydrocleys nymphoides* (Humb. & Bonpl. ex Willd.) Buchenau
Indian swampweed, Miramar weed	*Hygrophila polysperma* (Roxb.) T. Anderson
Dotted duckweed, dotted duckmeat	*Landoltia punctata* (G. Mey.) D.H. Les & D.J. Crawford
Asian marshweed, ambulia	*Limnophila sessiliflora* (Vahl) Blume
Creeping or sixpetal water primrose	*Ludwigia grandiflora* (Michx.) Greuter & Burdet ssp. hexapetala (Hook. & Arn.) G.L. Nesom & Kartesz [*Ludwigia hexapetala* (Hook. & Arn.) Zardini, Gu & P.H. Raven]
Uruguayan primrose-willow	*Ludwigia grandiflora* (Michx.) Greuter & Burdet spp. grandiflora (*Ludwigia uruguayensis* Camb.)
Moneywort, creeping jenny	*Lysimachia nummularia* L.
European wand loosestrife	*Lythrum virgatum* L.
Asian waterclover	*Marsilea minuta* L.
Australian waterclover	*Marsilea vestita* Hook. & Grev. (*Marsilea mutica* Fourn.)
European waterclover	*Marsilea quadrifolia* L.
Peppermint	*Mentha* ×*piperita* L. (pro sp.) [*aquatica* × *spicata*]
Asian spiderwort	*Murdannia keisak* (Hassk.) Hand.-Maz.
Parrot feather watermilfoil	*Myriophyllum aquaticum* (Vell.) Verdc.
European watermilfoil	*Myriophyllum spicatum* L.
Brittle waternymph	*Najas minor* All.
Sacred lotus	*Nelumbo nucifera* Gaertn.
Cape blue waterlily	*Nymphaea capensis* Thunb. var. *zanzibariensis* (Caspary) Conard
Yellow floatingheart	*Nymphoides peltata* (S.G. Gmel.) Kuntze
Ducklettuce	*Ottelia alismoides* (L.) Pers.
Cuban bulrush	*Oxycaryum cubense* (Poepp. & Kunth) Lye (*Scirpus cubensis* Poepp. & Kunth)
Water lettuce	*Pistia stratiotes* L.
Curly pondweed	*Potamogeton crispus* L.
Watercress	*Nasturtium officinale* W.T. Aiton [*Rorippa nasturtium-aquaticum* (L.) Hayek]
Giant arrowhead	*Sagittaria montevidensis* Cham. & Schltdl.
Common salvinia, water spangles	*Salvinia minima* Baker
Kariba-weed, giant salvinia	*Salvinia molesta* Mitchell
Salvinia	*Salvinia* spp. Ség.
Bigpod sesbania	*Sesbania herbacea* (Mill.) McVaugh
Bog bulrush	*Schoenoplectus mucronatus* (L.) Palla (*Scirpus mucronatus* L.)
Scrambling nightshade	*Solanum tampicense* Dunal
Exotic bur-reed	*Sparganium erectum* L.
Water chestnut	*Trapa natans* L.
European brooklime	*Veronica beccabunga* L.

Appendix B—Nonnative Invasive Plant Species Not to be Used or Recommended for Wildlife Food Plots nor Bird and Butterfly Viewing Gardens

There has been an explosion in the range of species and cultivars recommended, sold, and planted to enhance "wildlife food." Nonnative species are often recommended by Federal, State, and private game management agencies and organizations. As with gardening, imported species and wildlife seed mixes remain unregulated and are increasingly bred to be more vigorous, produce more fruit and seed, and be more immune to native predators. This is the common setup that enables some of these cultivars to become more aggressive and possibly invasive, even if they first appear benign due to the recognized lag phase. Nonnative species are often used because they are perceived to have "the upper hand" on native plant species that have coevolved with and supported the remaining wildlife and nongame fauna of southern ecosystems. Nonnative species are also used in an effort to restore disturbed sites, to compensate for plant-successional deficiencies in forested landscapes, and for nutritional deficiencies related to soil characteristics. The unbridled use of nonnative plants is a situation that is bound to degrade and pollute our native forests, wetlands, and grasslands.

Ideally, nonnative species should not be planted in forested areas. When using plant and seed catalogs, avoid those labeled "imported", "Asian", "European", "Siberian", or "exotic." Any nonnative seed established in a forest or grassland for specific game species has a good chance of escaping into surrounding habitat and permanently degrading its value for other wildlife species. Select plants and seeds native to your planting zone, or if possible, to your locale.

The following nonnative species are recognized invasive plants by one to several States or agencies in the Southeast (www.invasive.org/southeast/):

Trees

Russian olive	*Elaeagnus angustifolia* L.
Callery pear, Bradford pear	*Pyrus calleryana* Decne.
Sawtooth oak	*Quercus acutissima* Carruthers

Shrubs

Butterflybush	*Buddleja davidii* Franch.
Silverthorn, thorny olive	*Elaeagnus pungens* Thunb.
Autumn olive	*Elaeagnus umbellata* Thunb.
Surinam cherry	*Eugenia uniflora* L.
Winged burning bush	*Euonymus alatus* (Thunb.) Siebold
Largeleaf lantana	*Lantana camara* L.
Shrubby bushclover, bicolor lespedeza	*Lespedeza bicolor* Turcz.
Thunberg's lespedeza	*Lespedeza thunbergii* (DC.) Nakai
Japanese privet	*Ligustrum japonicum* Thunb.
Glossy privet	*Ligustrum lucidum* W.T. Aiton
Border privet	*Ligustrum obtusifolium* Siebold & Zucc.
Chinese privet	*Ligustrum sinense* Lour.
Privet	*Ligustrum spp.*
European privet, common privet	*Ligustrum vulgare* L.
Bell's honeysuckle	Lonicera ×bella Zabel [*morrowii × tatarica*]
Sweet breath of spring	*Lonicera fragrantissima* Lindl. & Paxton
Amur honeysuckle	*Lonicera maackii* (Rupr.) Herder
Morrow's honeysuckle	*Lonicera morrowii* A. Gray
Standish's honeysuckle	*Lonicera standishii* Jacques
Tatarian honeysuckle, twinsister's	*Lonicera tatarica* L.

continued

Appendix B—Nonnative Invasive Plant Species Not to be Used or Recommended for Wildlife Food Plots nor Bird and Butterfly Viewing Gardens (continued)

Shrubs (continued)

Macartney rose	*Rosa bracteata* J.C. Wendl.
Cherokee rose	*Rosa laevigata* Michx.
Multiflora rose	*Rosa multiflora* Thunb.
Himalayan blackberry	*Rubus armeniacus* Focke
Shrubby blackberry	*Rubus fruticosus* L. [excluded]
Wineberry, wine raspberry	*Rubus phoenicolasius* Maxim.
Linden arrowwood	*Viburnum dilatatum* Thunb.

Woody Vines

Japanese honeysuckle	*Lonicera japonica* Thunb.
Kudzu	*Pueraria montana* (Lour.) Merr.

Forbs

Chicory	*Cichorium intybus* L.
Coco yam, taro, elephant's ears	*Colocasia esculenta* (L.) Schott
Korean clover	*Kummerowia stipulacea* (Maxim.) Makino
Japanese clover	*Kummerowia striata* (Thunb.) Schindl.
Chinese lespedeza, sericea	*Lespedeza cuneata* (Dum. Cours.) G. Don
Black medick	*Medicago lupulina* L.
Burclover	*Medicago polymorpha* L.
White sweetclover	*Melilotus alba* Medikus, orth. var.
Yellow sweetclover	*Melilotus officinalis* (L.) Lam.
Sweetclover	*Melilotus* spp.
Wild radish	*Raphanus raphanistrum* L.
Cultivated radish	*Raphanus sativus* L.
Purple crownvetch	*Securigera varia* (L.) Lassen (*Coronilla varia* L.)
Rattlebox	*Sesbania punicea* (Cav.) Benth.
Garden vetch	*Vicia sativa* L.

Grasses and Grasslikes

Crested wheatgrass	*Agropyron cristatum* (L.) Gaertn.
Colonial bentgrass	*Agrostis capillaris* L.
Redtop	*Agrostis gigantea* Roth
Tall oatgrass	*Arrhenatherum elatius* (L.) P. Beauv. ex J. Presl & C. Presl
Yellow bluestem, King Ranch bluestem	*Bothriochloa ischaemum* (L.) Keng var. *Songarica* (Rupr. ex Fisch. & C.A. Mey.) Celarier & Harlan
Japanese bromegrass	*Bromus arvensis* L.
Rescuegrass	*Bromus catharticus* Vahl
Smooth brome	*Bromus inermis* Leyss.
Meadow brome	*Bromus racemosus* L.
Rye brome	*Bromus secalinus* L.
Bermudagrass	*Cynodon dactylon* (L.) Pers.
Purple nutsedge	*Cyperus rotundus* L.

continued

Appendix B—Nonnative Invasive Plant Species Not to be Used or Recommended for Wildlife Food Plots nor Bird and Butterfly Viewing Gardens (continued)

Grasses and Grasslikes (continued)

Orchardgrass	*Dactylis glomerata* L.
Barnyardgrass	*Echinochloa crus-galli* (L.) P. Beauv.
Indian goosegrass	*Eleusine indica* (L.) Gaertn.
Quackgrass	*Elymus repens* (L.) Gould
Weeping lovegrass	*Eragrostis curvula* (Schrad.) Nees
Centipede grass	*Eremochloa ophiuroides* (Munro) Hack.
Perennial ryegrass	*Lolium perenne* L.
Italian ryegrass	*Lolium perenne* L. ssp. *multiflorum* (Lam.) Husnot
Darnel ryegrass	*Lolium temulentum* L.
Dallisgrass	*Paspalum dilatatum* Poir.
Bahiagrass	*Paspalum notatum* Flueggé
Kodomillet	*Paspalum scrobiculatum* L.
Vasey's grass	*Paspalum urvillei* Steud.
Annual bluegrass	*Poa annua* L.
Kentucky bluegrass	*Poa pratensis* L.
Rough bluegrass	*Poa trivialis* L.
Tall fescue	*Schedonorus phoenix* (Scop.) Holub
Meadow fescue	*Schedonorus pratensis* (Huds.) P. Beauv.
Johnsongrass	*Sorghum halepense* (L.) Pers.

Appendix C—Low-Growing Native Plants with Potential for Southern Right-of-Way Stabilization and Beautification

These native plants are low growing and are recommended for stablizing roadside cut-and-fill banks and at the same time will add wildflower beauty. Seed sources are discussed in the text section, "Rehabilitation, Restoration, and Reclamation."

Forbs

Slender copperleaf	*Acalypha gracilens* A. Gray
Milkweeds	*Asclepias tuberosa* L. (*A. variegata* L.)
Downy pagoda-plant, horse mint	*Blephilia ciliata* (L.) Benth.
Spurred butterfly pea	*Centrosema virginianum* (L.) Benth.
Partridge pea	*Chamaecrista fasciculata* (Michx.) Greene, [*C. nictitans* (L.) Moench]
Butterfly-pea	*Clitoria mariana* L.
Ticktrefoil	*Desmodium strictum* (Pursh) DC., (*D. rotundifolium* DC.)
Poorjoe	*Diodia teres* Walter
Elephantsfoot	*Elephantopus tomentosus* L.
Catchweed bedstraw	*Galium aparine* L.
Carolina geranium	*Geranium carolinianum* L.
Pineweed	*Hypericum gentianoides* (L.) Britton, Sterns & Poggenb.
Smallflower morning-glory	*Jacquemonia tamnifolia* (L.) Griseb.
Lespedezas	*Lespedeza repens* (L.) W. Bartram, (*L. procumbens* Michx.)
Shaggy blazing star	*Liatris pilosa* (Aiton) Willd.
Littleleaf sensitive-briar	*Mimosa microphylla* Dryand
Evening primroses	*Oenothera speciosa* Nutt., (*O. fruticosa* L.)
Yellow woodsorrel	*Oxalis stricta* L.
Maypop passionflower	*Passiflora incarnata* L.
Largebracted plantain	*Plantago aristata* Michx.
Juniper leaf	*Polypremum procumbens* L.
Late purple aster	*Symphyotrichum patens* (Aiton) G.L. Nesom
Dollarleaf	*Rhynchosia reniformis* DC.
Pink fuzzybean	*Strophostyles umbellata* (Muhl. ex Willd.) Britton
Pencilflower	*Stylosanthes biflora* (L.) Britton, Sterns, & Poggenb.
Virginia tephrosia	*Tephrosia virginiana* (L.) Pers.
Tuberous vervain	*Verbena rigida* Spreng.

continued

Appendix C—Low-Growing Native Plants with Potential for Southern Right-of-Way Stabilization and Beautification (continued)

Grasses

Elliott's bluestem	*Andropogon gyrans* Ashe var. *gyrans*
Roundhead sedge	*Cyperus echinatus* (L.) Wood
Panicgrass	*Dichanthelium commutatum* (Schult.) Gould, [*D. aciculare* (Desv. ex Poir.) Gould & C.A. Clark], [*D. acuminatum* (Sw.) Gould & C.A. Clark]
Purple lovegrass	*Eragrostis spectabilis* (Pursh) Steud.
Pineywoods dropseed	*Sporobolus junceus* (P. Beauv.) Kunth
Virginia wild rye	*Elymus virginicus* L.

Vines

Yellow jessamine	*Gelsemium sempervirens* (L.) W.T. Aiton
Virginia creeper	*Parthenocissus quinquefolia* (L.) Planch.

Pesticide Precautionary Statement

Pesticides used improperly can be injurious to humans, animals, and plants. Follow the directions and heed all precautions on the labels.

Store pesticides in the original containers under lock and key—out of reach of children and animals—and away from food and feed.

Apply pesticides so that they do not endanger humans, livestock, crops, beneficial insects, fish and wildlife. Do not apply pesticides when there is danger of drift, when honeybees or other pollinating insects are visiting plants, or in ways that may contaminate or leave illegal residues.

Avoid prolonged inhalation of pesticide sprays or dust; wear protective clothing and equipment if specified on the label.

If your hands become contaminated with a pesticide, do not eat or drink until you have washed them. In case a pesticide is swallowed or gets in the eyes, follow the first aid treatment given on the label, and get prompt medical attention. If a pesticide is spilled on your skin or clothing, remove clothing immediately and wash thoroughly.

Do not clean spray equipment or dump excess spray material near ponds, streams, or wells. Because it is difficult to remove all traces of herbicides from equipment, do not use the same equipment for insecticides or fungicides that you use for herbicides.

Dispose of empty pesticide containers promptly and in accordance with all applicable Federal, State, and local laws.

NOTE: Some States have restrictions on the use of certain pesticides. Check your State and local regulations. Also, because registrations of pesticides are under constant review by the U.S. Environmental Protection Agency, consult your State forestry agency, county agricultural agent or State extension specialist to be sure the intended use is still registered.

www.ingramcontent.com/pod-product-compliance
Lightning Source LLC
Chambersburg PA
CBHW081219280526
45787CB00006B/2452